GW01046262

AFTE

AFTERMATH

Healing from the Trump Presidency

Karyne E. Messina, Ed.D.

PI Press

AFTERMATH: HEALING FROM THE TRUMP PRESIDENCY
PI Press, Chevy Chase, MD

© 2020 by Karyne E. Messina, Ed.D.

Cover image by Melonie Bell
Book design by Vinnie Kinsella

ISBN: 978-1-7362388-0-6
LCCN: 2021901213

Acknowledgments

I n the late eighties and early nineties, I learned a great deal about projective identification from David and Jill Scharff in a program they developed at the Washington School of Psychiatry. They piqued my interest in this phenomenon, leading to three decades of observation and study of this defensive maneuver that shifts blame from a projector to a recipient often blindsided by the intrusion. Little-known outside of psychoanalytic circles, projective identification is ever-present today, particularly in Washington, D.C. in 2020.

I thank the Scharffs for introducing me to this concept and for giving me the tools to raise awareness of projective identification since it touches people from all walks of life: from domestic abusers, bullies, and even racists who have relied on it for centuries to dominate others. Understanding projective identification is the first powerful step towards dismantling it and the various unfair systems propped up by it.

At the other end of the spectrum of human behavior is mentalization. I learned a great deal about this way of interacting from Jon Allan, to whom I am most grateful. Agreement is not required in this state of mind, but discussions between and among people with differing opinions are promoted in an atmosphere of respect.

I would like to thank Barbara Basbanes Richter who served as an excellent editor and helped me make esoteric concepts more understandable in a bid to encourage fellow Americans to move towards reconciliation and repair.

It is my hope that by recognizing the destructive nature of projective identification and by mentalizing—to promote discussions between and among people in an atmosphere of respect—we can find constructive ways to move forward for ourselves and for innocent children who deserve to live in a world without so much strife and acrimony.

Contents

Author's Note

This book was originally published in the fall of 2020 and thus refers to Donald Trump as the current president in some places. Understanding the scars he left on our country and how we can heal, however, remains notably topical.

INTRODUCTION

Our country is in a terrible state. The acrimony and cantankerousness that simmered during the months leading up to the 2016 presidential election morphed into bombast for some and dread for others once the ballots were counted. Since then, partisanship has only intensified—look no further than the September 2020 presidential debate between Donald Trump and Joe Biden—with communication among our representatives devolving into an intractability and viciousness rarely seen before.

The rest of us suffer as well. Our relationships weaken and sometimes fracture under the weight of our societal conflict; it feels impossible to move forward in a way that honors our own beliefs and also makes room for those with whom we don't see eye to eye.

By Thanksgiving of 2019, I was so concerned by the distress I was seeing around me that I decided then to do something about it. This book is my endeavor to contribute to the repair that is needed in our country. By using the knowledge and skills I have developed over three decades of treating patients for a wide range of psychological issues, I sincerely hope to present a tenable path forward, a clear route to healing in the aftermath of the destruction of the past four years.

My gravest concern is what is happening to the most vulnerable members of our society, our children. They are greatly influenced by most people in positions of authority, particularly the president, the person they see as being ultimately responsible for leading our country. Unfortunately, they are getting a strong message that not only is lying permissible, but so is lying about one's own ability to be truthful. They are also learning that promises and commitments are meaningless, whether they are made to other people or other countries; examples of magnanimity or generosity have all but vanished. What children are gleaning from this administration is that what's best for "me" is what counts. Further, because of the precipitous spread of disinformation, some children are learning the Earth is flat and has only been around for 5 millennia, and that Charles Darwin is the anti-Christ. Of course, children have always been susceptible to questionable information. Prior to the ubiquity of social media, kids regularly believed that swallowing a watermelon seed would cause vines to grow out of their ears, a myth that feels quaint to me now. Today, however, there are countless cases in which absolute lunacy is the new academic standard, as opposed to teaching children the truth about ourselves and our planet. That Earth has been around for 4.5 billion years is an undisputable fact, as is the future of a watermelon seed when it hits the stomach. The outcomes of both examples are not theories or hypotheses: they are facts.

In terms of our nation, many of the principles set forth by our Founding Fathers, including freedom and equality, are no longer being upheld; nor are the legacies of previous presidents, from Washington to Obama. Guidelines for how a person in the ultimate position of leadership and authority ought to conduct him- or herself is not the focus in the news in 2020. Instead, children see their peers being put into cages because they weren't born in the United States. They see families being split up while one or both parents are sent back to their country of origin, where they might face the possibility of torture or even death. They see mounting discrimination against women and people of color as well as anyone else who has different thoughts than President Trump and his followers. They see world leaders who counted on America to "do the right thing for humanity" turn to other countries for help because our head of state can no longer be counted on to keep his word. They also see an environment devastated at the fastest pace in recorded history: waterways polluted, air contaminated, and forests destroyed because of this administration's lack of concern about the future.

The warning signs of the Trump administration's departure from the goals set forth by the environmentally-sensitive Obama administration began on day one, when all references to climate change on the White House website were removed and replaced with calls for "energy independence."[1] Abrupt slashes to the Environmental Protection Agency's budget for domestic programs were also a portent of what was to come. Whether or not President Trump really believes the climate is changing in negative ways is unclear. What is obvious is that he has stated his beliefs, without showing he has adequate knowledge about the subject. Though hundreds, if not thousands, of scientists by now have shown there are most certainly definite connections between human activity and global warming, President Trump has decided not to heed their warnings.

An analogy comes to mind: Imagine that President Trump is told by expert engineers that a train is scheduled to come roaring down a railroad track at a particular time. Children are standing on that track and will remain there, unless told to move, until the exact time the train will pass through. Instead of immediately moving these children to a safer place, President Trump says the engineers have not provided incontrovertible "proof" that the train will indeed clamor through at the scheduled time. He chooses to ignore their warnings while letting them play continue in the same place. In this scenario, even if Trump knew the rail schedule and

---

1. Jolene Chreighton, "All Mentions of Climate Change Were Just Deleted From the White House Website," *Futurism*, January 20, 2017, https://futurism.com/all-mentions-of-climate-change-were-just-deleted-from-the-white-house-website

heard the train's whistle as it approached, he still wouldn't have the visible proof he thinks he needs to show the train's imminent harm to the children where they are standing. Of course, by that time it would be too late.

Whether moments, days, or years away, "incontrovertible" proof for things that are predicted to happen in the future is an impossibility. Yet we regularly avail ourselves of what makes the most sense: undertaking research on major issues, and consulting with experts and commission task forces, so people in charge can determine the facts in all areas that pose potential threats rather than ignoring what experts from around the world are saying. This is particularly important where there is a high likelihood that the results—whether those of a train running over children or the melting of icebergs—have irreversible consequences. One can't bring dead children back to life or refreeze melted icebergs, so why not seriously consider the life-altering warnings of experts instead of casting them aside?

While those recommendations by experts might seem reasonable enough, it is most unfortunate that President Trump, time and time again, says he *knows* things he has never studied. The audacity of this form of lying leads one to ask: Why does he do it? Is he not curious about the truth? Not having met him, I can't say I know for sure why he insists he is knowledgeable about things beyond his level of expertise. I do know, however, based on my years of experience as a psychologist and psychoanalyst that people who are not honest and truthful or, inversely, are so brazenly sure about what they know despite having little or no information, often boast about knowing "it all" out of insecurity.

I also know that people who are insecure often project things they don't like about themselves onto others and then act as if the problem resides within other people. This mental maneuver, which includes shifting blame to others, is something President

Trump does; a behavior that can be gleaned through observation of his written and spoken words.

In spite of the blatant disregard for human life, the lack of focus on environmental crises, and the paucity of regard for integrity, honesty and compassion, all qualities that may be receding into the background of society in many parts of America, we can all do something, in one way or another, to help counteract all that surrounds us in this time of crisis. If apathy as a state of mind or blind acceptance of what anyone says takes hold as the new normal in our country, we will confront even bigger problems than any of us know.

So, it is for the children of America that I write this book. I want them to know that people who cared about them tried in a number of ways to help counter the "Trump-effect" that is dismantling the core values of the United States. So, they will know there were people who tried—in all kinds of ways—to mitigate the incredible destruction that the Trump administration sowed in such a brief period of time. Only history will reveal how successful those opposed to the chaotic behavior of Donald J. Trump were.

CHAPTER ONE

Hurricane Trump

After five years of conditioning, the president's ceaseless lies, insults and abuse were no less breathtaking to behold. Mr. Trump doesn't care if you think he's corrupt, incompetent and self-centered. He just wants you to think everyone else is just as bad, and that he's the only one brave enough to tell it to you straight. It is an effort to dull Americans' sense of right and wrong, making them question reality itself and, eventually, driving them to tune out.

—Editorial Board, *The New York Times*, September 9, 2020.

I grew up in the Florida Keys where hurricanes were a frequent occurrence. In one storm that went through Marathon when I was a child, parts of bridges were severely damaged, houses were blown to smithereens, and seaweed filled the inside of my piano. As I recall, only the shoes I put on a cornice over the drapes in my house were not seriously damaged.

The hurricane itself was scary. The wind howled as I heard things outside crashing from one place to another. It felt as though my home was shaking like something that might be portrayed in a cartoon. I remember thinking this must have been what the three little pigs felt like as the big bad wolf blew their houses in. It seemed to me that day that my world was coming apart as frightening images of destruction filled my mind. I even imagined what it would be like to die in a storm.

The winds died down after a few hours, followed by an eerie calm. This was the eye of the hurricane. The worst was yet to come. Within thirty minutes, the winds returned, howling with a vengeance. We heard the exploding of the transformers being struck by lightning, and soon our house was bathed in darkness. Each minute felt like an eternity. That was the darkest night I could recall spending in the Keys. At one point, we retreated to the bathroom because rainwater was seeping into the living room, but soon enough, seawater gurgled up through the toilet. I thought we might drown.

Eventually, near dawn, the storm moved on. The water in the bathroom receded to the sea. The outlines of the sun were finally visible. Soon, the rain stopped.

By daybreak, the storm had finally blown away, and we emerged from our home to assess the damage. Our car was flattened by a fifty-five-foot palm tree. The yard was flooded with several feet of standing water. We waded through the chest-high water that had fully submerged my yard towards the center of the beach highway, through water that creeped up to my chest. I saw fish swimming along with toys and other objects torn from their homes.

This hurricane flattened a great deal of the Keys. Once the winds subsided, the National Guard set up tent shelters, creating a sea of plastic blue tarps. We were unable to leave our house for another three days, during which time we were still without running water and electricity. Our food stores dwindled, but we were lucky—we still had a roof over our heads. We did what we could to help neighbors who had lost everything. There was a sense of togetherness that was invigorating despite the massive destruction.

In a strange twist of fate, my parents had been entertaining houseguests when the storm hit. Luckily, their car had survived the storm with minor dents and dings, and they had had the good sense to top off their gas tank when they arrived in town. Since no gas pumps from Marathon to Miami were working and our car was destroyed, it was a stroke of luck that our friends had a workable car with nearly a full tank of fuel. It was time to abandon ship. Our houseguests invited us to join them on their trip back to their home in Washington, DC.

I stayed longer than my parents, perhaps a little over a month. When they returned to Marathon to repair the house, I finished out the rest of the summer with my aunt, Maryanne Alexander, in Alexandria, Virginia. Never again did we tempt fate by staying in the Keys during a storm of that intensity. Nature won.

I left the Keys for good after I turned eighteen. After receiving my bachelor's degree in Florida, I attended graduate school in Washington, D.C. Interestingly, my Aunt Maryanne helped me get an interview with the newly appointed director of a facility for handicapped people, future D.C. mayor Vincent Gray. I worked for Vince and discovered a deep love and appreciation for my adopted city that hasn't changed since.

Presidents came and went. No one was perfect, and they all made mistakes as well as doing good for the country. It wasn't until the 2016 election results were official that those same dreadful feelings that I had experienced during the frightening storm of my youth resurfaced.

Donald Trump roared into Washington like a hurricane. He wrecked structures as well as agreements that had taken years to put into place and that many experts considered necessary for the good of our country and our planet. He withdrew from the Paris Climate Agreement, pulled out of the Iran nuclear deal, and left the UN Human Rights Council, to name only a few disruptive changes. To make matters worse, he did these things without having experience with or expertise in the areas these agreements covered.

Hurricanes are a part of nature that can't be controlled, but Donald J. Trump is man-made. That said, it is important to point out that everyone has *not* experienced this administration in the same way that I have—plenty of Americans have benefitted from tax breaks and business incentives pushed through by the Trump administration. Nevertheless, however great the differences in opinion may be, we must find ways to talk about what has occurred and how to move forward as one country while listening to and learning from various viewpoints. It is through discussions about our differences and active listening in an atmosphere of respect that we will eventually be able to return to the more reasonable way of navigating in a democracy.

As a psychologist and psychoanalyst, the weeks after the presidential election of 2016 were very difficult for me. During patient sessions, I sat with people devastated by the results of the election. Many cried, others were deeply depressed, while still others were gripped by fear of what was to come.

Since 2016, I've spent lots of time thinking about the president, his behavior, and how he treats friends and foes. It's clear to me that President Trump is an expert projective identifier—don't worry, I will explain what that is below—but in short, he is someone who manages to find fault with others rather than himself. It's always the other guy who's wrong, or lying, or cheating. Think of all the epithets Trump uses to describe his opponents: "Crooked Hillary"; "Sleepy Joe"; "Lyin' Ted"; "Little Marco." By making someone else the bad guy, Trump offloads the perception of himself onto the target of his verbal assignation.

I believe Trump's behavior is encouraging the development of a generation of people inclined to hateful identity politics and bigotry, while also dismantling our country's institutions and natural resources. But this book is not a left-leaning jeremiad against Trump; rather, this book is intended as a guide on how we can heal, with ideas on how each of us can help bridge the divide that has only grown deeper since Election Day in November 2016, due in part to the way Donald Trump constantly shifts blame, which is known in psychoanalytic circles as *projective identification*.

Coined by psychotherapist Melanie Klein in 1946 to describe a theoretical, unconscious process that happens in infancy, which was later expanded to describe a type of defense mechanism that occurs in adulthood, *projective identification* refers to a phenomenon employed by people who unconsciously dislike something about themselves. Instead of taking responsibility, they blame those feelings, thoughts, or actions on others.

This happens all the time and at all social levels.

To heal will take time, patience, and a willingness to pull our heads out of the sand, take stock of our viewpoints, and square them with divergent ones. It's not so unusual anymore for families and friends who find themselves on opposite ends of the political spectrum to refrain from engaging in any sort of meaningful conversation for fear that such discussions will ruin already fractured relationships. And that's fair—I've seen plenty of families, unfortunately, who are no longer able to be in the same room with each other.

The media has capitalized on this, too; who among us hasn't seen headlines screaming clickbaity titles like "How to survive Thanksgiving with your Never Trumper family," or "My lost Christmas weekend with my MAGA in-laws"? Generally, these how-to guides advise meditation, peacekeeping—anything to avoid talking about the issues that are the most pressing and in need of discussion. Further, when these stories do suggest broaching political topics, the advice is often provided from a combative viewpoint, nearly guaranteeing that whoever is starting the conversation will be perceived as a know-it-all bent on educating the hapless pupil.

Consider this advice from Elie Mystal, executive editor of AboveTheLaw.com, who said on MSNBC's *All In with Chris Hayes* in August 2019 that "you do not negotiate" with Trump's white supporters. A story that appeared in a 2017 issue of *Harper's Bazaar* suggested that divorce was the only option if a couple found themselves on opposite ends of the political divide. Think about it: who among us appreciates being lectured to as though we're toddlers or combatants on the battlefield? No one. And the thought that total separation is the only way forward is downright depressing.

Unfortunately, self-selection among political groups means that there's very little, if any, communication with people who have different beliefs, and when some of us are faced with a different point of view, it's attacked. If you're a liberal, you're an elite wanna-be one-percenter thumbing your nose at the "deplorables," while conservatives are portrayed as dyed-in-the-wool Americans with traditional—some might say prejudicial—values that just don't jibe with the twenty-first century. Whatever your beliefs are, you probably don't like being painted with such an unforgiving brush, but that's where we are. Though this polarization did not start with Trump, his combative nature has normalized the tendency to oversimplify situations and attack those who dare to disagree.

However, all is not lost. We can make progress, heal the divide, and learn from each other. I'll be sharing my personal political viewpoints here, and yes, full disclosure, I am a Democrat. But I do not want that to turn you away—in fact, I hope you'll stick around and see how I think we can make our different backgrounds our country's greatest strength.

Misogyny and Projective Identification—Shifting Blame to Feel Better

Projective identification happens all the time—think of the "mean girls phenomenon," where a group will gang up on one girl for no outwardly obvious reason. That's an example of projective identification. Sometimes, someone who is acutely uncomfortable with a feeling or thought will want to dispose of it, but how do you dispose of a feeling? Enter *projective identification*—the act of shifting blame onto someone else. And, on some level, the process works: the person shifting the blame feels better, and, in some cases, the recipient senses something is off but isn't quite sure what the issue is. No harm, no foul, right? Not exactly: as the perpetrator continues to project onto the same person or groups of people, the victim becomes acutely aware that something is wrong. Even worse, the victim may come to believe these nasty untruths.

These days, another type of blame-shifting frequently takes place over social media. Let's say a girl branded with a bad reputation claims via Twitter or Instagram that another girl has had sex with lots of boys in school, unlocking a painful series of events. Initially, the labeled girl may feel stunned by the accusation. However, when she is shunned, ridiculed, and dropped by her friends, the victim may begin to question herself. She might start to feel badly about herself, which can fuel the beginnings of depression. This girl may also experience feelings of hopelessness, culminating with thoughts that include some type of self-harm. Making suicidal gestures or even attempting suicide can result in cases when severe depression emerges.

Refusing to let another person have his or her own thoughts is a form of blame-shifting. When a person projects his or her unwanted thoughts onto someone else and accuses that someone else of having those thoughts, it causes the innocent person to feel stunned and confused. The projector—whom I will refer to as the bully in this book—continues to monitor the other person to control him or her to make sure he or she still has those thoughts. It is as if the bully takes control of the victim's own thoughts, and, in some severe cases, this is exactly what happens.

Bullies are often guilty of blame-shifting. For example, a bully might call someone a "loser." Why? Oftentimes, bullies are victims of abuse themselves—perhaps someone in the bully's life has called him or her a loser, and it makes the bully feel bad. Rather than find a positive or constructive way to deal with those bad feelings, the bully passes on those negative feelings to someone else. The person being called a loser may feel confused at the outset. However, before long, the victim may believe the bully and decide that, yes, the bully is right. The victim is indeed a bona fide loser. When this occurs, the receiver is identifying with the thought or feeling that the projector sought to dispel.

Basically, bullies aren't happy with themselves. They were probably bullied at one point, but who wants to feel like a victim of a bully? People find various ways to cope. Some people internalize those feelings, others may find someone to talk to, but some may look to another person to blame—someone who's even scrawnier, less outgoing, less intelligent, less whatever—and that way, the bully doesn't feel like he's the loser. Instead, it's that other kid over there. The bully blames the other person by getting people to look at him or her; he or she is the one that is dumb or stupid or can't play ball.

The process of blame-shifting can happen in a split second, and though the recipient might feel stunned initially, over the course of repeated attacks, those thoughts may begin to feel real, especially since bullies generally pick on the same people over and over. Subconsciously, bullying ensures that the victim still represents those negative feelings the bully is trying to dispel.

Blame-shifting can happen within a romantic relationship, too: say one partner is the so-called "sloppy" one. When he was a kid, his room was a mess and his parents were always after him to clean up. Then he grows up, gets married, and his wife believes he's still the sloppy one. "Look at this house!" she'll exclaim. "It's a mess. You are so sloppy." When things go well between two people, the husband will accept these projections.

However, if the husband realizes one day that he's only half of the problem, he might say to his wife, "Well, look, we're both less than perfect—just look at your closet, there are clothes everywhere!" This case isn't so toxic—it's annoying, but it is quite common and easily solved.

Unfortunately, that rarely happens on its own. More often, relationships built on blame-shifting tend to deteriorate. Abusive relationships are often constructed on this pattern of behavior. Consider the example of a husband who mistreats his wife. The relationship likely didn't start with abuse. Perhaps he showered her with gifts and praise, but once the honeymoon was over, the mask came off; now, the husband shows his true colors and is petty, selfish, and authoritative. He hits her, he belittles her, and yet, she refuses to leave—this story is so well-known that it's become a cliché. Why doesn't she leave? She must know she deserves better. Perhaps, deep down, she does, but the persistent emotional degradation eventually takes its toll. He says she's bad or worthless, and eventually she comes to believe it. In some cases, the woman not only believes that she is flawed but is also the root of the blame—it is her fault that she is so awful and that she is beaten by her husband.

In cases of physical abuse, perpetrators often blame victims for something they themselves think or do. Instead of taking responsibility for their own actions, they accuse the other person of bad behavior they claim must be corrected.

In the case of domestic violence, battered women often come to believe what they've been told by their abusers: "No one will ever want someone like you," "You're lucky I like you," or "You're a pathetic person. No wonder you disgust me." From the outside, it seems so clear—of course the victim isn't at fault—but after years of mistreatment, the mind grows weary and submits rather than fights. Accepting the blame can become a survival instinct.

Trump and His Treatment of Women

The way Trump talks to and about women is a form of blame-shifting. Let's look at his face-offs with Hillary Clinton in the lead-up to the 2016 presidential election. On the surface, Trump bullied Clinton by calling her names, leading chants of "lock her up" at his political rallies, and pacing the stage like a world-champion pugilist during the October 2016 presidential debate. By most accounts, someone who seems to enjoy mocking others is generally considered a bully.

The process of blaming Hillary Clinton freed Trump from unpleasant feelings or notions about himself. Trump likely felt a sense of relief each time he lashed out at Clinton. Calling her a liar and a crook dispelled the notion that, deep down, he may believe it is *he* who is a liar and a crook. It's also possible that Trump has read and heard stories about himself calling him these things, and rather than address those issues straight on, Trump projects those ideals onto others. Further, by consistently referring to Clinton as a liar and a crook, Trump probably fully believes that she is those things. Clinton is a crook, full stop.

I believe that Trump shifted his insecurities about women in power onto Hillary Clinton in verbal attacks that hardly subsided once the election results were tallied. And Trump's unseemly behavior towards women hardly began or ended with Clinton; in 2015, Trump engaged in a nearly year-long spat with Republican commentator and then-journalist for Fox News, Megyn Kelly. As usual, Trump turned to Twitter to vent after what he felt was a line of unfair questioning by Kelly, claiming that he had been targeted more than other candidates at the debate:

Wow, @megynkelly really bombed tonight. People are going wild on twitter! Funny to watch.[2]

Then, during an interview later that day on CNN, Trump continued the tirade against Kelly, saying, "You can see there was blood coming out of her eyes, blood coming out of her wherever." Trump later tweeted that he was referring to Kelly's nose, rather than her menstrual cycle.

Trump's obsession with bleeding women didn't stop with Kelly. In June 2017, MSNBC *Morning Joe* co-host Mika Brzezinski mocked Trump on air for displaying a fake *Time* magazine cover featuring his likeness at some of his properties. In retaliation, Trump took to Twitter on June 29, 2017, writing that during a visit to his home at Mar-a-Lago over New Year's Eve, Brzezinski's face was bleeding, allegedly due to a facelift. In a 1993 interview with Howard Stern, Trump claimed to be a germaphobe and that he washes his hands as often as possible. In his 1997 book, *The Art of the Comeback,* Trump writes that "one of the curses of American society is the simple act of shaking hands."

Trump has also claimed to be disgusted by facial blemishes and once scrapped a television advertisement because one of the women in the ad had a mole on her face. In burst of rage Trump screamed, "Did you see that? Did you see that? I don't believe this. She's ugly!" He apparently was extremely outraged. "This is shit. This girl is a three for chrissakes! How could you have a girl with a face that's flawed in my commercial."[3]

---

2. @realDonaldTrump, 2:40 am, Aug 7, 2015, https://twitter.com/realdonaldtrump/status/629557762427604992?lang=en

3. John R. O'Donnell, James Rutherford, *Trumped: The Inside Story of the Real Donald Trump—His Cunning Rise and Spectacular Fall,* Crossroad Press, 2016.

Coupled with Trump's obsessive-compulsive symptoms, this fear of germs and contagion, disgust of facial blemishes, and demand for perfection would seem to suggest that Trump becomes highly anxious when any of these conditions exist—just look at how he's handled the Covid-19 crisis—but his fear of germs most likely includes blood on one's face because its presence implies damage somewhere, that imperfection exists and that loss of control of one's body is evident. And, since germs, imperfection, and loss of control all scare Trump, he projects these conditions onto others, which in turn frees him of these fears, at least temporarily. To ensure that these fears remain away, he monitors those imperfections to make sure they continue to reside in his chosen victim.

In December 2017, Trump suggested that Senator Kirsten Gillibrand had traded sex for campaign contributions:

> Lightweight Senator Kirsten Gillibrand, a total flunky for Chuck Schumer and someone who would come to my office "begging" for campaign contributions not so long ago (and would do anything for them), is now in the ring fighting against Trump. Very disloyal to Bill & Crooked-USED![4]

In other words, powerful women cannot possibly earn their place by virtue of hard work—they must sleep with even more powerful men instead. Trump's tweet suggests that Gillibrand is unprofessional and capable of little more than seducing unsuspecting men.

Even wives of political opponents have been subject to Trump's tirade. During the presidential campaign, Trump tweeted that then-GOP candidate Carly Fiorina had no chance of winning

---

4. @realDonaldTrump, December 12, 2017, https://twitter.com/realdonaldtrump/status/940567812053053441?lang=en

because she was ugly: "Look at that face!" he wrote. "Would anyone vote for that?" Trump even tweeted side-by-side photos of his wife Melania and Heidi Cruz, wife of senator and onetime presidential candidate Ted Cruz, suggesting that Cruz was ugly:

@Don_Vito_08: "A picture is worth a thousand words" @realDonaldTrump #LyingTed #NeverCruz @ MELANIATRUMP[5]

As an avowed germaphobe, these comments about women and

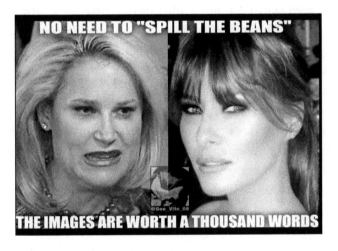

blood are surprising, but after considering the depths Trump is plumbing to share these thoughts, these misogynistic outbursts are more than just the acts of a bully. Trump is a blame-shifter—and we the people are paying the price. When the president cannot control his emotions and projects his innermost insecurities onto others, the behavior loses its shock value. We become desensitized to what is otherwise abhorrent behavior.

5. https://twitter.com/realdonaldtrump/status/712850174838771712?lang=en

Trump's blame-shifting appears to be a lifelong pattern of behavior that shows no signs of abating. In January 2020, *Real Clear Politics* reported that Trump accused Nancy Pelosi of being a "crazed lunatic." At the same time, the House of Representatives had impeached Trump and the Senate was wrapping up its trial. Meanwhile, *The Washington Post* has been keeping track of Trump's misleading or false statements, and as of July 2020 there are over 20,000 of them. So, for Trump to say Pelosi is, "a crazed lunatic" and that "She will go down as I think maybe the worst speaker in the history of our country" are statements similar to those that have been said about him. Rather than consider these unsavory statements, Trump shifts these accusations onto Pelosi to make her the damaged, bad, and incompetent person who will go down in history as the worst Speaker of the House of Representatives. In this way, he can rid himself of being accused by many as the "worst president in history."

And despite his treatment of others, we cannot forget that President Trump appeals to many Americans—perhaps you are among the 40 percent of the country who think he's great. Though my personal feelings are different, I do not want to discount that, and I don't want to talk down to those who support him.

Rather, understanding how blame-shifting works and how the current president employs it will demonstrate that this is a common phenomenon and that there are ways to turn around the negativity.

The Case for Common Language

Though rooted in psychoanalysis, this book attempts to get at the essence of projective identification and how we can combat its prevalence in order to reach the goal of speaking with one another without villainizing one another. In the pages that follow, I'm going to use common language about how Trump's behavior is having consequences for us as a society. I will also provide ideas for moving forward and how we can once again engage in thoughtful, meaningful debate from opposite ends of the political rainbow.

Psychoanalysis should not be cloistered in the elite ivory towers of academia—most people would greatly benefit from understanding how the mind works and why we act the way we do. Important terms known only to a handful of psychoanalysts could help make a real difference in the lives of many people if only they were part of everyday language. One term that definitely falls into this category is *projective identification*, as defined at the beginning of this chapter and which I will refer to throughout the book as blame-shifting. Another term in this category is *mentalization* which is instrumental in helping bullies and their victims overcome the ugly cycle of abuse. Unfortunately, these terms are intimidating, which is why I will illustrate them throughout the book with real-life examples and sample dialogues.

Beyond these pages, I suggest that there are groups of people who promote the principles that are inherent in *mentalization* without using the word itself.

The mental health community has a responsibility to help and to do no harm. I believe that our patients would be better served if we could come together as a professional community and update powerful words and concepts to allow people to understand what is happening to all of us in our divisive and divided world.

Further, I think writers, authors, journalists, and therapists have a duty to use clear and precise language so everyone can understand the destructive forces that are in play. We must demand that our leaders engage in a process that incorporates a respectful way of communicating between and among people.

A Word on Psychoanalysts Analyzing the President—Is It Ethical?

There has been a lot of talk about whether it is right or even ethical for psychologists to publicly discuss the mental state of a sitting president, and as a psychoanalyst, I know this may seem like treading in unchartered waters. I am not the president's psychoanalyst and am not attempting to diagnose his mental state. Instead, I am offering my opinion based on what I have observed from afar and on my nearly three decades of experience working with traumatized patients. I am not *diagnosing* President Trump. As an expert in the field of psychoanalysis, I am highlighting what could be his defense mechanisms, and I am doing this by listening to what Trump says on TV as well as what I have read in newspapers and magazine articles. It's important to note here that we all have defense mechanisms—we certainly couldn't navigate the world without them—but it appears that those Trump employs are wreaking havoc on nearly everyone around him—and that includes the American people.

Some People Won't Change

Certainly, some people don't want to change, even if the problem they're facing interferes with the routine of their daily lives. No one can intervene unless the person in question wants to take that first step. This is especially true when someone is suffering from a mental health issue which many professionals have suggested.

Think of the obnoxious alcoholic uncle who embarrasses his family with his drunken outbursts and boorish behavior. He doesn't see his alcoholism as a problem. In this case, the alcoholic may recognize that he has a problem, but it doesn't bother him enough to seek treatment.

However, let's imagine another obnoxious alcoholic uncle who recognizes that his drinking disturbs his family a great deal and wants to change; here, there is hope for change. This person may seek treatment of some type because his problem bothers *him* in addition to bothering those around him.

Members of Trump's base may simply not be ready to talk or listen. They believe that Trump is doing great things for them and for the country. Some of these people will not want to reach across the aisle, and that's okay. But I don't think that means the dialogue has to stop, so long as a respectful attitude is maintained. Where things get blurry is when people refuse to accept that certain behaviors are not okay when they previously would have objected to them on moral or legal grounds. In cases like this, I think it is important to try and point out the discrepancies whether you are heard or not—more on just how to do that in Chapter Eight.

Misogynists are often given a free pass because that's just how they are—let boys be boys, right? I disagree. Rather than writing off misogyny, we can say things like "Joe, I find what you just said to be offensive and disparaging. You can say what you wish, but please don't do it in my presence." Words are powerful—let's relearn how to use them to our benefit.

CHAPTER TWO

Assessing the Damage,
Understanding the Source

*The present rate of production of carbon dioxide from fossil
fuel combustion is about a hundred times the average rate
of release of calcium and magnesium from the weathering
of silicate rocks. As long as this ratio holds, precipitation of
metallic carbonates will be unable to maintain an unchang-
ing content of carbon dioxide in the atmosphere. Within a
few short centuries, we are returning to the air a significant
part of the carbon that was slowly extracted by plants and
buried in the sediments during half a billion years.*[6]

—*Restoring the Quality of Our Environment: Report of
the Environmental Pollution Panel,* President's Science
Advisory Committee, November 1965

*Brutal and Extended Cold Blast could shatter ALL
RECORDS. Whatever happened to Global Warming?*

—Donald J. Trump, tweeting @realDonaldTrump,
November 21, 2018[7]

As the Vietnam War raged, President Lyndon B. Johnson
received a startling report written by some of America's
top scientists. The topic was not weapons or chemical
warfare, but rather how humans were rapidly baking planet Earth.

---

6. Roger Revelle, Wallace Broecker, et al. *Restoring the Quality of Our Environment: Report
of the Environmental Pollution Panel,* November 1965. https://carnegiedge.s3.amazonaws
.com/downloads/caldeira/PSAC,%201965,%20Restoring%20the%20Quality%20of%20
Our%20Environment.pdf

7. https://twitter.com/realDonaldTrump/status/1065400254151954432

In *Restoring the Quality of Our Environment*, climate scientists Roger Revelle, Wallace Broecker, and others warned that "Man is unwittingly conducting a vast geophysical experiment. Within a few generations he is burning the fossil fuels that slowly accumulated in the earth over the past 500 million years... The climatic changes that may be produced by the increased CO2 content could be deleterious from the point of view of human beings. The possibilities of deliberately bringing about countervailing climatic changes therefore need to be thoroughly explored."[8] The team predicted the melting of the Antarctic ice caps, rising sea levels, warming of the oceans, increased acidity of water, and other catastrophic events.

To his credit, Johnson, who by 1965 had already signed the Clean Air Act into law two years prior, shared the disturbing report with the public. And the various conservation measures he enacted did improve air and water quality—we can thank him for reducing air pollution by 50 million tons since 1970—but he did not have the solutions necessary to tackle the admittedly daunting task of reducing carbon emissions.[9] Subsequent presidents also addressed visible signs of pollution while the larger invisible threat grew unchecked.

To say that it's infuriating to see the can kicked down the road is an understatement—those fifty-year-old predictions that stunned Johnson are now coming to pass—and it's clear that previous administrations chose to defer action on this issue rather than address it. Unfortunately, President Trump is the man at the helm right when these disasters are manifesting themselves, and he

---

8. Revelle, 126-7.

9. National Park Service U.S. Department of the Interior, Lyndon B. Johnson National Historical Park, "Lyndon B. Johnson and the Environment," accessed February 13, 2020, https://www.nps.gov/lyjo/planyourvisit/upload/EnvironmentCS2.pdf.

is neither willing nor prepared to address this issue, or at the very least acknowledge its existence. His dismissal of existing scientific data is dangerous for the citizens of this country for whom the effects of climate change are already at hand. Trump's denial of accepted facts is not limited to the environment—since leaping into the Manhattan real estate scene in the 1970s, Trump has played with the facts to suit his needs, whether that's discussing the source of his wealth or the size of his intellect.

Trump and his advisors have politicized climate change and other issues, while Trump's expert ability of shifting blame has altered how we communicate with each other. These behaviors have made it nearly impossible to have an open and honest dialogue about present and future environmental issues since even basic facts have been called into question under Trump's presidency, such as whether climate change even exists. When facts are less important than ideology, there's little room left for finding middle ground and even less hope of finding solutions that we all need, no matter where we fall in our political beliefs—we're all breathing the same air, after all.

What follows is a brief outline of the history and significance of climate change and how Trump's blame shifting is sowing havoc. I could have easily replaced this topic for another—immigration, tax reform, or civil rights—but the point here is not to make a case for the issue, but to demonstrate how an expert manipulator has denied decades of research to suit his own political agenda.

Climate Change and Policy

According to the National Oceanic and Atmospheric Administration (NOAA), January 2020 in the United States was the fifth warmest in the 126 years since recording began, and the ninth consecutive January with temperatures above the twentieth century average. Above-average precipitation soaked the Midwest, while severe thunderstorms ravaged the South, bringing with them tornadoes and heavy rains that saturated the soil and paved the way for an increased risk of flooding come springtime. [10]

By increasing the temperature of our oceans, climate change is leading to more intense hurricanes and tropical storms. The effects of tropical cyclones are numerous and well known. Stronger winds and heavier rains can cause severe flooding and destruction, which are predicted to occur with greater regularity through the twenty-first century. More powerful storms will also require more remediation efforts, which will be costly: according to the Center for Climate and Energy Solutions, eight of the ten costliest hurricanes on record in the United States have occurred since 2004, each resulting in billions of dollars in damage. [11]

In 2016, the EPA released a paper entitled "Climate Change Indicators" and opened with searing lines echoing those written by President Johnson's climate scientists in 1965:

> The Earth's climate is changing. Temperatures are rising, snow and rainfall patterns are shifting, and more extreme climate events—like heavy rainstorms and record high temperatures—are already taking place. Scientists are highly confident that many of these observed changes

10. NOAA National Centers for Environmental Information, State of the Climate: National Climate Report for January 2020, published online February 2020, retrieved on February 12, 2020 from https://www.ncdc.noaa.gov/sotc/national/202001.

11. C2ES, Center for Climate and Energy Solutions, Hurricanes and Climate Change, published online 2020, retrieved on February 12, 2020 from https://www.c2es.org/content/hurricanes-and-climate-change/.

can be linked to the levels of carbon dioxide and other greenhouse gases in our atmosphere, which have increased because of human activities. [12]

Humans have been adding greenhouses gasses into the atmosphere at an increasing rate since the Industrial Revolution. The amount currently trapped in our atmosphere is at a staggering 401 ppm—a 43 percent increase over levels initially observed in the late 1700s. For comparison, the last time this much CO2 was in our atmosphere was approximately 3 million years ago. None of this is the result of conspiracies carried out by a "Deep State;" in fact, thank French mathematician Jean Baptiste Joseph Fourier (1768-1830) for discovering the greenhouse effect in the 1820s. In *Théorie Analytique de la Chaleur (1822)* Fourier offers this introduction to the properties of heat conduction:

> Heat, like gravity, penetrates every substance of the universe, its rays occupy all parts of space. The object of our work is to set forth the mathematical laws which this element obeys. The theory of heat will hereafter form one of the most important branches of general physics… [13]

Then, in mathematical pirouettes based on Newton's law of cooling, Fourier provides a fundamental equation for heat

12. EPA Environmental Protection Agency, Climate Indicators in the United States, fourth edition, published August 2016, retrieved on February 12, 2020 from https://www.epa .gov/sites/production/files/2016-11/documents/climate-indicators-2016-fact-sheet.pdf.

13. Jean Baptiste Joseph Fourier, translated by Andrew Freeman, *The Analytical Theory of Heat.* Cambridge, 1878. https://books.google.com/books?id=No8IAAAAMAAJ&printsec =frontcover&dq=theorie+analytique+de+la+chaleur&hl=en&newbks=1&newbks _redir=0&sa=X&ved=2ahUKEwi9oPW5rsznAhXsRt8KHXaiAoIQ6AEwAnoE CAYQAg#v=twopage&q=heat%2C%20like%20gravity&f=false.

conduction and deduces that Earth's atmosphere acts like an insu-
lator and that what gets trapped inside it heats the planet as well.
The term "greenhouse effect" is not his, however; thank Swedish
meteorologist Nils Gustaf Ekholm for conjuring that in 1901.[14]

Climate change as a policy matter in the United States can
be traced to the 1950s, but the recent history of climate change
policy only really dates to April 1993 when president Bill Clinton
announced he would sign a treaty protecting endangered species
and follow a timetable to reduce carbon dioxide emissions. He
even proposed a general energy tax on all forms of energy and
carbon pollution.[15] Despite intense backlash, a fuels tax did pass,
but was hardly as broad as the original proposal. And, Clinton
vowed to bring carbon dioxide emissions to 1990 levels by the
year 2000, but obviously we've blown right past that deadline.
The problems we face now have been predicted for years, but we
might all feel better about humanity's chances to correct course if
there weren't a climate change denier in the White House.

If Trump were merely a passive climate change denier, then
perhaps his inaction couldn't possibly be any worse for our country than the various panaceas applied by previous presidents.
Rather, he is actively pressing the notion that climate change
is a fallacy. In a tweet from March 12, 2019, Trump quoted a
climate sceptic who misrepresented himself as a co-founder of
Greenpeace: "Patrick Moore, co-founder of Greenpeace: 'The
whole climate crisis is not only Fake News, it's Fake Science.
There is no climate crisis, there's weather and climate all around

14. Ekholm, Nils, 1901. On the Variations of the Climate of the Geological and Historical
Past and Their Causes. *Quarterly Journal of the Royal Meteorological Society.* vol. 27. 1-61.
http://nsdl.library.cornell.edu/websites/wiki/index.php/PALE_ClassicArticles/archives
/classic_articles/issue1_global_warming/n5._Ekholm__1901.pdf

15. Carbon Tax Center. History. Accessed February 12, 2020. https://www.carbontax
.org/history/.

the world, and in fact carbon dioxide is the main building block of all life.' @foxandfriends. Wow!"[16] Greenpeace quickly issued a counter tweet saying that, "Patrick Moore was not a co-founder of Greenpeace. He does not represent Greenpeace. He is a paid lobbyist, not an independent source." (Moore's relationship with Greenpeace is itself long and murky, but Moore remains very much persona non grata with the organization.) But the damage was done: Trump's initial tweet was retweeted 32,000 times and liked by 100,000 followers. Greenpeace's response was retweeted 10,000 times. Actively denying climate change is irrational and done at the expense of our existence as we know it.

This stance is a significant pivot from what Trump the private citizen believed on climate change: on December 6th, 2009, he, along with children Ivanka, Donald Jr., and Eric, were among the dozens of signatories to a public full-page letter that ran in *The New York Times* to president Obama imploring him to tackle climate change (see next page).

That plea appeared to be little more than a publicity stunt. Trump changed his mind shortly thereafter when he began tweeting in earnest about how climate change is a joke. In 2013, he wrote that an "Ice storm rolls from Texas to Tennessee - I'm in Los Angeles and it's freezing. Global warming is a total, and very expensive, hoax!"[17] To ring in 2014, he wrote "This very expen-

16. Donald J. Trump. "Patrick Moore…" March 12, 2019. Accessed February 13, 2020, https://twitter.com/realDonaldTrump/status/1105445788585467904?ref_src=twsrc %5Etfw%7Ctwcamp%5Etweetembed%7Ctwterm%5E1105445788585467904&ref_url =https%3A%2F%2Fwww.cnn.com%2F2019%2F03%2F12%2Fus%2Ftrump -climate-change-tweet-patrick-moore%2Findex.html.

17. Trump, December 6, 2013, accessed February 13, 2020, https://twitter.com/realDonald Trump/status/408977616926830592?ref_src=twsrc%5Etfw%7Ctwcamp%5Etweet embed%7Ctwterm%5E408977616926830592&ref_url=https%3A%2F%2F www.motherjones.com%2Fenvironment%2F2016%2F12%2Ftrump-climate-time line%2F.

THE NEW YORK TIMES, SUNDAY, DECEMBER 6, 2009

Dear President Obama & The United States Congress,

Tomorrow
leaders from 192 countries
will gather at
**The UN Climate Change Conference
in Copenhagen**
to determine
the fate of our planet.

As business leaders we are optimistic that President Obama is attending Copenhagen with emissions targets. Additionally, we urge you, our government, to strengthen and pass United States legislation, and lead the world by example. We support your effort to ensure meaningful and effective measures to control climate change, an immediate challenge facing the United States and the world today. Please don't postpone the earth. If we fail to act now, it is scientifically irrefutable that there will be catastrophic and irreversible consequences for humanity and our planet.

We recognize the key role that American innovation and leadership play in stimulating the worldwide economy. Investing in a Clean Energy Economy will drive state-of-the-art technologies that will spur economic growth, create new energy jobs, and increase our energy security all while reducing the harmful emissions that are putting our planet at risk. We have the ability and the know-how to lead the world in clean energy technology to thrive in a global market and economy. But we must embrace the challenge today to ensure that future generations are left with a safe planet and a strong economy.

Please allow us, the United States of America, to serve in modeling the change necessary to protect humanity and our planet.

In partnership,

Chris Anderson, Curator, TED   Richard Baker, Chairman, Lord & Taylor   Dan, David & Lauren Barber, Blue Hill   Chris Blackwell, Founder, Island Records, Island Outpost   Graydon Carter, Editor, Vanity Fair   Deepak Chopra, Adjunct Professor, Kellogg School of Business and Management   Yvon Chouinard, Founder, Patagonia   Ben Cohen, Jerry Greenfield, Co-founders, Ben & Jerry's   Gregory Colbert, Creator, Ashes & Snow   Kenneth Cole, Chairman, Kenneth Cole   Paulette Cole, CEO & Creative Director, ABC Home, ABC Carpet & Home   Tom Colicchio, Chef & Owner, Craft Restaurants   Kit Crawford, Gary Erickson, Co-Owners & Co-CEOs, Clif Bar & Company   Steve Ells, Founder, Chairman & Co-CEO, Chipotle Mexican Grill, Inc.   Eileen Fisher, CEO, Eileen Fisher   Walt Freese, CEO, Ben & Jerry's Homemade   Mitchell Gold, Chairman, Bob Williams, President, Co-Founders, Mitchell Gold + Bob Williams   Matt Goldman, Co-Founder & CEO, Blue Man Group   Seth Goldman, CEO, Honest Tea   Robert Grabler, Founder, Poisonobe Associates, Jenga Licensor   Adrian Grenier, Reckless Productions   Alan Hassenfeld, former Chairman, Hasbro, Inc.   Don Hazen, Executive Editor, AlterNet   Gary Hirshberg, CEO, Stonyfield Yogurt   Jeffrey Hollender, CEO, Seventh Generation   Kate Hudson, David Babali, Co-Founders, David Babali for WildAid   Mike Kaplan, CEO, Aspen Skiing Company   Michael Kieschnick, President, Credo Mobile   Sheryl Leach, Creator & Founder of Barney   Sven-Olof Lindblad, Founder, Lindblad Expeditions   Danny Meyer, CEO, Union Square Hospitality Group   Laura Michalchyshyn, President & GM, Planet Green, Discovery Communications   Will Raap, Chairman & Founder, Gardener's Supply Company   Horst Rechelbacher, Founder, Aveda, Founder & CEO, Intelligent Nutrients   David Rockwell, Founder & Owner, Rockwell Group   Maury Rubin, Founder, Chef & CEO, City Bakery, Birdbath Green Bakery   Michael Rupp, CEO & President, The Rockport Company   Gordon Segall, Chairman, Crate & Barrel   Jeff Skoll, Founder, Participant Media and Skoll Foundation   Harvey Spevak, CEO, Equinox   Greg Steltenpohl, Founder, Odwalla   Michelle Stein, President, Aeffe USA   Martha Stewart, Founder, Martha Stewart Living Omnimedia, Inc.   Jeffrey Swartz, CEO, Timberland   Tom Szaky, CEO, TerraCycle   Donald J. Trump, Chairman and President, Donald J. Trump Jr., EVP, Eric F. Trump, EVP, Ivanka M. Trump, EVP, The Trump Organization   Jean-Georges Vongerichten, Executive Chef & Owner, Jean-Georges Management LLC

if you want to go quickly, go alone. if you want to go far, go together. african proverb

Business leaders, sign onto this initiative: businessleaders4environmentalchange.us

sive GLOBAL WARMING bullshit has got to stop. Our planet is freezing, record low temps, and our GW scientists are stuck in ice."[18] But Trump wasn't yet president, and so these tweets were largely toothless.

Once in the Oval Office, however, Trump's tweets took on new meaning. On December 7th, 2016, Trump named former Oklahoma attorney general Scott Pruitt to lead the Environmental Protection Agency, a notable selection given Pruitt's record of suing the EPA to block President Obama's Clean Power Plan. During an interview with CNBC in 2017, Pruitt said that he did not believe carbon dioxide to be "a primary contributor to the global warming that we see."[19] And prior to his resignation in 2018 after being dodged by various ethics violations,[20] Pruitt worked to roll back environmental protections in the name of job growth, including a proposal to weaken fuel economy standards for vehicles and pushed to abandon the Paris Climate Treaty. In what appeared to be an attempt to obfuscate the facts on climate change, the EPA's 2014 Climate Change Adaptation Implementation Plan was removed from that agency's website the day Trump was inaugurated. A copy of the document was uploaded to DocumentCloud by NPR reporter Rebecca Hersher and is freely available online to whomever wishes to view it.

---

18. Trump, January 1, 2014, accessed February 13, 2020, https://twitter.com/realDonald Trump/status/408983789830815744?ref_src=twsrc%5Etfw%7Ctwcamp%5Etweetembed %7Ctwterm%5E408983789830815744&ref_url=https%3A%2F%2Fwww.motherjones .com%2Fenvironment%2F2016%2F12%2Ftrump-climate-timeline%2F.

19. Tom Christopher, "EPA chief Scott Pruitt says carbon dioxide is not a primary contributor to global warming," March 9, 2017, accessed February 13, 2020, https://www.cnbc .com/2017/03/09/epa-chief-scott-pruitt.html.

20. Rebecca Herscher, "EPA Chief Pruitt Faces Mounting Scrutiny For Ethics Violations," April 3, 2018, accessed February 13, 2020 https://www.npr.org/2018/04/03/599145343/epa -chief-pruitt-faces-mounting-scrutiny-for-ethics-violations.

Pruitt replacement is former coal lobbyist and fellow climate denier Andrew Wheeler, who is continuing the agenda of his predecessor by removing and weakening regulations on water and air pollution.

Ok, what does all this have to do with a book on blame-shifting? Trump is charismatic—he understands how to talk to people and assure them that he is listening to them. And he is speaking to more than the stereotypical base of white, poor, uneducated American men. Throughout his campaign and even during his presidency, Trump has cast himself as an outsider, that he is leading the people against a vast, frightening government conspiracy trying to force Americans to comply with burdensome programs. As such, his claims and his lies become irrelevant when wrapped up in theories of hijacked freedom and the American way. Data becomes meaningless and his stories about how cold the weather is or that climate change is a Chinese hoax are far more reassuring and relatable than the ominous threats of a warming planet. A lack of facts also allows Trump to weaponize misinformation and hurl it at those who would question him or debunk him with data.

It also helps Trump's cause that we are in the midst of an era when Americans are more inclined to doubt science—consider, for example, parents who refuse to vaccinate their children for fear of catching autism, even though there is no link between the two.[21] A recent Gallup poll found that the number of Americans who believe vaccines are important fell from 94 percent in 2001 to 84 percent in 2019. And though the majority of respondents said that vaccines are less dangerous than the diseases they prevent, 46 percent said they were unsure whether vaccines caused autism—down from 52 percent from Gallup's last poll in 2015,

---

21. Centers for Disease Control and Prevention, National Center for Emerging and Zoonotic Infectious Diseases (NCEZID), Division of Healthcare Quality Promotion (DHQP) Page last reviewed: October 27, 2015. Accessed February 13, 2020. https://www.cdc.gov/vaccinesafety/concerns/autism.html

but still high enough to suggest that misinformation continues to influence the decision-making process.[22]

Trump's political rhetoric appeals to Americans who felt their needs were ignored by other Republican politicians and previous administrations. Even before Trump was considered a serious presidential contender, change was afoot in the United States with a chasm growing ever wider between the urban coastal areas and the Midwest.

The financial crisis of 2008 paved the way for people to flock to Trump and his chant of "Make America Great Again." The meltdown that pushed the global economy to the brink of disaster had well-documented effects on Americans from all social and economic backgrounds. An in-depth report by the *Wall Street Journal*'s Gerald Seib found that the wounds left by the Great Recession cut deep, and many never fully healed. Seib suggests that the trauma turned members of both parties against globalization and towards a sense of retrenchment:

> The recession didn't merely inflict pain across much of the country. For those on both the left and right it generated deep new skepticism about whether the country's financial and political establishments really are interested in conducting the country's affairs for the benefit of all.
>
> More than that, many average Americans concluded the establishment's reaction to the crisis, once under way, was insufficient in light of the pain inflicted.[23]

---

22. RJ Reinheart, "Fewer in US Continue to See Vaccines as Important," Gallup, January 4, 2020, accessed on February 13, 2020, https://news.gallup.com/poll/276929/fewer-continue-vaccines-important.aspx.

23. Gerald Seib, "How the U.S. Became a Nation Divided," *The Wall Street Journal*, December 17, 2019, https://www.wsj.com/articles/how-the-u-s-became-a-nation-divided-11576630802?mod=searchresults&page=1&pos=20

A surge of undocumented immigrants entered the country and ended up in communities unaccustomed to newcomers. Hostility brewed in the heartland, while left-leaning Americans saw the reluctance to embrace immigrants as a thinly veiled excuse for overt acts of racism and discrimination. Conservative voters believed Obama was too moderate, too distanced from those in Middle America. The shift to Donald Trump during the presidential campaign of 2016 was subtle, but his team capitalized on this simmering discontent and exploited it. While many, admittedly left-leaning Americans thought Trump's bid for the presidency was merely a publicity stunt, Trump successfully harnessed the anger and fear of those who felt forgotten and brought it to the fore. Trump did not belittle his base, but he listened, and he gave voice and power to their rage.

While running against Hillary Clinton for the presidency, Trump painted his opponent as an elite, out of touch snob who did not visit the Rust Belt states because she didn't think it was worth her time. And, to her detriment, Clinton paid little more than lip service to some states while completely ignoring others. Consider Wisconsin: since Obama won the state twice, Clinton and her team believed that state would remain Democrat. In reality, blue collar workers there felt ignored. Trump seized on that opportunity and harnessed that anger into an electoral triumph.

I interviewed one of Clinton's friends who stumped for her during the 2016 election. The source, who asked to remain anonymous, offered to answer my questions to help me determine the validity of my hypothesis: that angry blue-collar voters turned to Trump as their valiant savior. The source confirmed that Democrats had overlooked those states where Trump knew he could gain popularity. "Saying that Hillary was going to continue Obama's legacy did not convey what she had intended," the source said. "Some of those folks didn't like Obama, so that was not what they wanted to hear. People lost their jobs, they didn't believe the economy was improving, employment rates didn't seem right to them—rather, people dropped out of the market because they haven't been able to get jobs." Additionally, the idea that "black lives matter" was not well received, and not heard as intended by those who feel ignored.

In short, Clinton's friend said a "confluence of energies" led to the upset. For example, he said that "Hillary cares deeply about veterans and their families, I know she does, but plenty of veterans are mad at her, which is hard to explain." Unlike her husband Bill, she did not make an active show of feeling voters' pain. Her messaging targeted those who were already going to vote for her but only infuriated those who were suffering in the heartland. In a game of inches, Trump covered the field and won.

Clinton did not lose the popular vote—she lost in the Electoral College. Electoral votes are based on the National Census, and every state receives votes equal to its senators and congressional representatives, totaling 538 electors in all. The magic number to securing the presidency is 270 electors. [24] George W. Bush bested Al Gore in a similar fashion in the 2000 election. The electoral college also favored Rutherford B. Hayes in 1876 and Benjamin Harrison in 1888 without the popular vote.

Voters are not casting ballots for a candidate, but rather for their electors to vote for a candidate. So, someone's vote from a highly populous state like New Jersey will count less than a vote cast by someone in a less populated state like Wyoming, which ultimately leads to misrepresentation in the electoral college.

Trump visited voters in states like Wyoming, Wisconsin, and

---

24. National Archives, "Electoral College: Distribution of Electoral Votes," last reviewed December 23, 2019. Accessed February 24, 2020. https://www.archives.gov/electoral-college/allocation.

Missouri, and connected with blue-collar, Rust Belt workers frustrated with the way the economy was turning. Conservative columnist Michael Barone put it best in a December 2016 editorial when he offered advice to Democrats licking their wounds and wondering where it all went wrong:

> To recover, Democrats need to take a look at the map. The relevant map in this election divides the nation between coastal America (the West Coast plus Hawaii, as well as the Northeast from Maine to Washington, D.C.) and heartland America (the South, the Midwest and the Mountain West, as well as energy states Alaska and Pennsylvania). Coastal America casts 31 percent of popular votes and 170 electoral votes. Heartland America casts 69 percent of popular votes and 368 electoral votes.[25]

Many of those Americans living in Heartland America are white conservatives. Trump took the side of white conservatives, and they have not forgotten. They remain loyal to him just as he has continued to tell them that he is their champion—even when the facts don't bear that out. Trump says he will bring back jobs in manufacturing sectors, and though that doesn't look like it's going to happen, people still believe him. They overlook plant closures in Detroit and elsewhere in exchange for bombast and rhetoric that soothes acute short-term pain. The Trump methodology of disavowing facts has also involved the systematic dismantling of traditional media, a task originally delegated to Trump's former chief strategist, Steve Bannon. Facts become irrelevant when they are manipulated and fabricated. And when those traditionally

---

25. Michael Barone, "Some Free Advice for the Democratic Party," *RealClear Politics*, December 13, 2016, accessed February 24, 2020, https://www.realclearpolitics.com /articles/2016/12/13/some_free_advice_for_the_democratic_party_132547.html.

charged with providing the facts—i.e., journalists—are labeled the enemy, the average American feels adrift. Bannon achieved this by bombarding the average American with so much conflicting information that ultimately it would not matter whether the information was true or false. The goal was to put people in a constant state of unease and distrust. And by making the media the enemy, who could the average American trust? In an interview with *The New York Times* in 2017, Bannon said that "The media here is the opposition party. They don't understand this country. They still do not understand why Donald Trump is the president of the United States."[26] Trump has repeated the trope, calling members of the media among some of the most dishonest people on earth. And after hearing that on a constant loop, people begin to doubt themselves—maybe *The New York Times* reporters are out to get the president? How do we separate fact from fiction?

Newspapers have not always presented fair and equitable viewpoints—indeed, many media outlets throughout history were founded with the very purpose of sharing a particular viewpoint—but for decades there has been an understanding that though a news provider may have a conservative or liberal slant, usually reserved for the editorial pages, the reported content is true and accurate. Some scholars even argue that 20th-century fairness and accuracy in reporting is something of an anomaly in the history of the media, and the breakdown of objective reporting is merely a return to historical norms.[27] Today, with the

26. Michael Grynbaum, "Trump Strategist Steven Bannon Says Media Should 'Keep Its Mouth Shut,'" *The New York Times*, January 26, 2017, accessed February 13, 2020, https://www.nytimes.com/2017/01/26/business/media/stephen-bannon-trump-news-media.html.

27. Heidi Tworek, John Maxwell Hamilton, "Why the 'golden age' of newspapers was the exception, not the rule," Neiman Lab, Harvard University, May 2, 2018, accessed February 13, 2020, https://www.niemanlab.org/2018/05/why-the-golden-age-of-newspapers-was-the-exception-not-the-rule/

proliferation of social media and the ability for anyone with an internet connection to become an independent journalist, facts no longer matter.

In this environment, people are emotional wrecks and perfectly primed to respond to someone who claims to understand their distress and has a plan to fix it. People gravitate towards others who are charismatic and confident.

A Disintegration of American Values

Trump is hardly the country's first divisive president. Andrew Johnson, America's seventeenth president, is widely considered to have been grossly incompetent in his role of reuniting the country in the months and years after the Civil War. Because of his incompetence in office and his incredible miscalculation of the extent of public support for his policies, Johnson is judged by historians as a great failure in securing a satisfying and equitable peace. Scholars have pegged him as a rigid, dictatorial racist unable to compromise or to accept a political reality at odds with his own beliefs. For example, rather than forging a compromise between radical Republicans and moderates during his presidency, his actions united the opposition against him. Johnson's opposition to the Freedmen's Bureau Bill (a bill that would have provided shelter for former slaves as well as their rights in court), the Civil Rights Act of 1866, and the Fourteenth Amendment eliminated the hope of repairing the country. In the end, Johnson did more to extend the period of national strife than he did to heal the wounds of war.

Most importantly, Johnson's unwavering commitment to ob- structing political and civil rights for black Americans played a large role in the failure of Reconstruction and the government's inability to solve the race problem in the South. Johnson's decision to support the return of the prewar social and economic system—except for slavery—dashed any hope of an equitable restricting of society in the South.[28]

It's possible that Andrew Johnson exhibited projective identification, too: Consider this statement he made to the federal commissioner of the Public Buildings Service:

> Everyone would, and *must* admit, that the white race was superior to the black, and that while we ought to do our best to bring them . . . up to our present level, that, in doing so, we should, at the same time raise our own intellectual status so that the relative position of the two races would be the same.[29]

By making such a statement, Johnson *may* have been projecting his own feelings of inferiority: Johnson was born into poverty and did not attend school. If he could shift his feelings about his lack of education on black Americans, he could rid himself of his inferiority complex, at least temporarily.

Remember, projective identification—or "blame shifting," as we're calling it in this book—is a defense mechanism, usually an unconscious one, that people employ to rid themselves of intolerable personality traits. It is a powerful defense mechanism. In the process, these qualities are shifted onto another person, who often feels stunned, and not sure what has just taken place.

---

28. Elizabeth Varon, "Andrew Johnson: Impact and Legacy," Miller Center at UVA. 2019. https://millercenter.org/president/johnson/impact-and-legacy

29. David Preiss, *How a Difficult, Racist, Stubborn President Was Removed From Power—If Not From Office*, Politico, November 13, 2018, accessed February 25, 2020. https://www.politico.com/magazine/story/2018/11/13/andrew-johnson-undermined-congress-cabinet-david-priess-book-222413

Eventually, however, the victim may believe these characteristics are true, which can lead to a host of issues.

In the following scenario pieced together from real examples I've heard in my practice, a woman we'll call Jessica explains an episode in which she is the victim of projective identification. During one abusive episode, Jessica recalled how her boyfriend "Jason" verbally berated her:

> "He yanked my purse out of my hand, opened it, and threw everything on the floor while calling me a stupid, greedy tramp," Jessica said. She was stunned and felt numb and didn't know what was happening. She said she was afraid to breathe. "Jason went on ranting and raving, saying I had robbed him of everything he'd ever had in life." Jessica sat down on a pillow he had thrown on the floor. Her body was shaking. As the rant continued, she tried to figure out what led to this outburst as she sat trying to pretend she was a statue. She feared interrupting Jason as he continued to depict her as a despicable character. Soon Jessica began to wonder whether she was indeed a dishonest and bad person. Had she stayed out too late? Did she talk to her friends too much?

In this scenario, Jason is shifting his feelings about himself onto Jessica. Jason believes deep down that he is dishonest, despicable, and unreliable, but rather than dealing with those feelings himself, he has found a more palatable solution by charging his girlfriend with these epithets instead. Now, Jason feels better, but what about Jessica? As the abuse continues, Jessica internalizes these words and comes to believe that yes, she is as deplorable as Jason says she is.

Projective identification can happen to women and men at all levels of society—we saw it at work between Trump and Hillary

Clinton, it happens in abusive relationships, and there are historical examples as well.

In public, Eleanor Marx, the youngest, English-born daughter of philosopher Karl Marx, was a pioneering feminist who championed the working downtrodden. In private, she found herself at the mercy of a bully.

Though largely unknown outside academic circles today, Eleanor Marx helped give voice to social feminism and organized labor. After her father's death in 1883, Marx took up his mantle, traveling around the world and spreading the word of the coming workers' revolution. Right around the time of her father's death, Marx became romantically involved with a fellow atheist named Edward Aveling, a married biology professor and Darwin disciple whom she met in the British Museum's reading room.

By the next year, the relationship turned serious, and Marx and Aveling were living together but could not wed because Aveling said he could not divorce his wife. In a letter to her friend Dottie Radford, Marx writes, "I am going to live with Edward Aveling as his wife. You know he is married, and that I cannot be his wife legally, but it will be a true marriage to me—just as much as if a dozen registrars had officiated...."[30]

Aveling proved, in the short term, at least, to bring out the best in Marx, boosting her confidence in her ability to speak to crowds and bend the ears of politicians and other movers and shakers. In public, they were an unmissable, united front. Away from prying eyes, however, Aveling became petty, jealous, and nasty. He had expensive tastes in clothing, cars, and nights on the town, and racked up debts all over London. Letters acknowledging his inability to repay friends are now in the British Library. But

---

30. Letter from Elanor Marx to Dollie Radford, June 30, 1884, Add MS 89029-1-25. Western Manuscripts, The British Library.

rather than leave the debts unpaid, Aveling's beloved Eleanor covered his bills.

Further, Aveling often disappeared at a moment's notice—taking "the cure" in a far-off locale, usually in the company of another woman—and regularly left Marx alone and in the dark about his whereabouts. In March of 1898, Marx learned that a year earlier, Aveling had married a twenty-two-year-old actress named Eva Frye under an assumed name. This news came on the heels of six months Marx spent caring for Aveling, who by then was suffering from kidney disease. On March 31, Marx was discovered dead in her bedroom. The cause? Ingestion of prussic acid, obtained from a local pharmacist. Interestingly, the initials on the note to the pharmacist were Aveling's but whether Marx had forged his name or whether Aveling purchased the poison remains unclear.

And what of Aveling? He inherited Marx's estate which he spent with abandon until his own death four months later. Marx's relationship with Aveling is a little-known but excellent example of projective identification. Like many people who find themselves victims of this cycle, Marx probably had no idea what was happening to her at the outset—perhaps a suspicion that her boyfriend was a jerk, but not much more than that. As the abuse escalated, it would have been difficult for Marx to ignore his behavior, but she pushed aside those nagging thoughts, preferring to live in ignorance than face the truth. Marx probably wanted to believe Aveling was a good and honest person—she nursed him back to health after discovering he was married to a younger woman; she paid his debts and accepted his mistreatment until his betrayals could no longer be ignored.

Marx's solution—if she did indeed commit suicide—need not be the answer for those caught in the cycle of blame shifting. For a victim to heal, there must be a willingness to confront the bully and to engage in difficult conversations. It is the only way for victims to heal and for bullies to stop shifting blame onto others. With concentrated effort, it is possible to heal and to recover. I'll talk about how this is done shortly.

CHAPTER THREE

American Children, Morality, and the Trump Administration

When our children are young, we work doggedly to foster in them a deep and abiding sense of morality, ethics and character. We try to teach them to always tell the truth, to be kind and generous, to be brave enough to do the right thing even if others aren't as brave. We try to teach them empathy and compassion, that caring about the less fortunate betters society and is also self-edifying. We teach them to be gracious and thankful and not to brag or bully. Also, don't lie, cheat or steal...And, Trump is teaching them that you can be the worst version of yourself, rise to the most powerful position in the world and scare people into not holding you accountable.[31]

—Charles M. Blow, opinion columnist for
The New York Times, July 17, 2019

As many people believe, children are like sponges; they absorb so much information and all sorts of social cues when they are young, whether it is learning a new language or learning what is considered proper behavior towards others. And they naturally—and often unconsciously—imitate those around them, trying on the behavior they see in others for size until, eventually, that behavior becomes their own.

With that in mind, authority figures and adults in leadership positions, including the president of the United States, serve as role models for the next generation. They are expected to lead by

---

31. Charles M. Blow, "What Trump Is Teaching Our Children," *The New York Times*, July 19, 2019, https://www.nytimes.com/2019/07/17/opinion/trump-american-children.html.

example, demonstrating through word and deed those universal values such as truthfulness, compassion, and kindness towards others.

It is alarming then, on many levels, when a president or other figure of authority lies, makes misleading statements, bullies opponents and perceived enemies, and leans into hyperbole and braggadocio, as Donald Trump has. The example he sets can normalize that same ugly behavior in children, which, in turn, may lead to an entire generation predisposed to violent outbursts and bullying rather than conflict resolution and active listening.

President Trump, His Lies, and Their Effect on Children

As mentioned earlier, for years, the *Washington Post* has maintained a database entitled "The Fact Checker: The Truth Behind The Rhetoric," keeping a tally of the number of false or misleading claims made by politicians. The Fact Checker has been particularly busy since President Trump assumed office. In three years—from January 20, 2017 to January 19, 2020—the number of lies or misleading statements made by Trump has climbed to 16,241.[32] When averaged out over the course of those three years, that's nearly fifteen lies a day (the number has now jumped to over 20,000).

It is worth noting that each type of lie is given equal weight. Trump's hyperbolic claims that he's "never had an empty seat" (which were likely never meant to be taken so literally) are treated the same as his misleading insults directed toward Speaker of the House Nancy Pelosi.[33]

---

32. Glenn Kessler, "The Fact Checker: The Truth Behind The Rhetoric," Updated January 19, 2020, https://www.washingtonpost.com/graphics/politics/trump-claims-database/.

33. Glenn Kessler, "The Fact Checker: The Truth Behind The Rhetoric," Remark made November 22, 2019, http://wapo.st/trumpclaimsdb?claim=14837.

Misleading or not, some adults write off Trump's lies as his modus operandi and nothing more: *He's a New York businessman! This is how they all talk, right?* To others, however, those same statements may provoke anxiety and anger. Additionally, while well-informed adults may be able to distinguish between a relatively harmless exaggeration and the more pernicious insults and misleading or false policy statements, these misleading or false statements and insults can have a deleterious effect on children who are simply too young to detect the vagaries of nuance in speech. They are still impressionable, still learning about morality and how it is to be exercised in society.

Therefore, when Donald Trump repeatedly makes false or misleading assertions, when he does not treat his words with care or a level of precision befitting the office of the president of the United States, he is teaching children through example that anything goes. That it is okay to say anything, to lie, even, if it serves their interest. And since Trump doesn't seem to suffer any consequences for his actions beyond a tongue-lashing from Democrats and pundits every now and then, children may feel invincible and beyond reproach. And this could leave a subtle and long-lasting impression on America's youngest generation.

Indeed, a wealth of data culled from recent studies shows the effects that lies—even small ones—have on children. In a 2014 study, for example, researchers at the University of California at San Diego explored whether an adult's lie would, in turn, make an elementary or preschool-aged child more inclined to lie. A total of 186 children were split into two groups. One group was told by an adult that there was a bowl of candy in the next room. But once the children arrived, the adult admitted that the candy was just a ploy, and instead, she wanted the child to play a fun game with her. The other group was only told about the fun game in the next room; there was no mention of candy.

The children then played a guessing game: based only on a catchphrase ("Tickle Me" for Elmo, for instance) or some other sound, they were asked to identify a stuffed toy. After two easier rounds, the researcher played the third clue, Beethoven's "Für Elise," then excused herself from the room to answer a phone call, telling the child not to peek—not surprisingly, most, but not all, gave into temptation. Upon the researcher's return, the children were asked to promise to tell the truth—had they peeked? If so, would they lie about the transgression?

The findings are illuminating. Those who had been lied to at the beginning of the experiment were more likely to peek *and* more likely to lie about peeking than those who had been told the truth. In addition, elementary-aged children were more likely to lie than preschool-aged children. The researchers concluded that:

> [G]iven that the children not only lied more if they had been lied to but also peeked more, it is likely that the children were doing more than simply imitating the modeled behavior. Perhaps these children made assumptions about the importance of honesty to the model. This would explain why the children who were lied to were more dishonest in general, and would be consistent with data suggesting that children's social imitation can influence their moral judgments (Bandura & McDonald, 1963). Another possibility is that rather than imitating, the children were extracting information about the adult who lied to them, and then using that information to decide how to respond. Perhaps the children did not feel the need to uphold their commitment to tell the truth to someone whom they perceived as a liar.[34]

---

34. Hays, Chelsea & Carver, Leslie. (2014). Follow the liar: The effects of adult lies on children's honesty. Developmental Science. 17. 10.1111/desc.12171. https://www.research gate.net/publication/260837765_Follow_the_liar_The_effects_of_adult_lies_on_child ren's_honesty.

The results of this research highlight other behaviors that go beyond mere imitation. Children may be able to intuit how much an adult values honesty, thus internalizing that same value (or lack thereof) and applying that concept to their own still-evolving worldview: *If that person thinks it is acceptable to lie, it must be acceptable for me to lie, too.* Additionally, trust and trustworthiness cut both ways. Children may feel less inclined to be honest to those who have lied to them, which, in turn, weakens their ability to form a strong moral code independent of external forces.

A second study, conducted by Nanyang Technological University in Singapore, continues the exploration into how being lied to as a child affects adulthood. A total of 379 Singaporean young adults were surveyed and asked to self-report whether their parents lied to them as children, how often they currently lie to their parents, and how well- or maladjusted they believe themselves to be in adulthood.

While there are inherent limitations in self-reported surveys, the findings reveal a possible connection between being lied to as a child and lying to parental figures. In addition, those who reported being lied to as a child were more likely to report "higher levels of psychosocial maladjustment...including externalizing problems, internalizing problems, and psychopathic attributes."[35] Externalizing problems included behaviors such as increased aggression or an inclination towards rule-breaking; internalizing problems, on the other hand, included feeling anxious, depressed, or withdrawn.

These studies illustrate how even relatively minor lies (e.g., the lie about candy in the next room) to children can contribute to an erosion of trust, the effects of which can reverberate into

35. Setoha, Peipei, Siqi Zhao, Rachel Santos, Gail D. Heyman, Kang Lee (2019). Parenting by lying in childhood is associated with negative developmental outcomes in adulthood. Journal of Experimental Child Psychology. Volume 189, January 2020,104680. https://www.sciencedirect.com/science/article/pii/S002209651830540X?via%3Dihub.

adulthood and contribute to other behavioral issues. However harmless they may appear, the lies parents tend to default to, like that there are no replacement batteries for a toy when they are simply sick of hearing the sounds play on repeat[36], may have more of an effect than we'd like to believe.

Applied to a high-profile authority figure such as President Trump, this calls into question the consequences of even his obvious exaggerations—whether or not they were intended to be taken literally. Imagine, then, the harm that can be inflicted by larger, more pernicious lies, especially when they are uttered or perpetuated by those who are highly respected or in positions of power.

Bullying and the Trump Effect

A nationwide survey found that approximately 20 percent of students between the ages of twelve and eighteen experienced bullying at school during the academic year in 2017. This is down from 29 percent in 2005. Interestingly, however, the decline has generally leveled off since 2015 with one exception: there was an increase in the percentage of students in rural areas who have experienced bullying (from 18 percent in 2015 to 27 percent in 2017).[37]

I will add that Donald Trump received higher levels of support in the 2016 election from voters in these same, predominantly rural communities. Just 12 percent of Trump voters said they lived in an urban setting, whereas 35 percent lived in a rural area.

---

36. @thedad, April 2, 2018, https://twitter.com/thedad/status/980837486065782785.

37. "Indicator 10: Bullying at School and Electronic Bullying," Indicators of School Crime and Safety, National Center for Education Statistics, Updated April 2019, https://nces.ed.gov/programs/crimeindicators/ind_10.asp.

The percentages among Clinton voters are nearly the reverse: 32 percent were located in urban areas, and 19 percent were from a rural area.[38]

A separate study examined the prevalence of bullying in the Virginia school system since the 2016 presidential election. Three surveys were conducted—in 2013, in 2015, and in 2017—that focused on students' experiences with bullying in the seventh and eighth grades. Those results were then compared to the election results for each school district. In districts Donald Trump carried, 18 percent more students reported having been bullied than in those districts Hillary Clinton carried. Moreover, a higher percentage (9 percent) reported that students were bullied due to their race or ethnicity.[39]

This study was undertaken as a result of reports that bullying has been more prevalent in the years since Donald Trump became president. It is careful to point out that the results did not suggest an uptick post-election but does seem to support the argument that bullying in specific areas of the country is increasing. Furthermore, anecdotal evidence from across the country seems to bear this conclusion out and adds perspective to these statistics.

In Ohio in 2016, two kindergarteners were overheard telling a Latino classmate that he would be sent back to Mexico as a result of Trump's presidency.[40] More recently, in rural Williamson

38. "An examination of the 2016 electorate, based on validated voters," Pew Research Center, AUGUST 9, 2018, https://www.people-press.org/2018/08/09/an-examination-of-the-2016-electorate-based-on-validated-voters/.

39. Huang, F. L., & Cornell, D. G. (2019). School Teasing and Bullying After the Presidential Election. Educational Researcher, 48(2), 69–83. https://doi.org/10.3102/0013189X18820291.

40. Marjorie Cortez, "Trump presidency worrisome to immigrants, refugees," *Deseret News*, November 9, 2016, https://www.deseret.com/2016/11/9/20600141/trump-presidency-worrisome-to-immigrants-refugees.

County, Tennessee, middle-school students locked arms and pretended they represented a wall on the border—a key campaign promise from Donald Trump's 2016 presidential run. Nonwhite students were not permitted to pass their human barricade.[41] A recent *Washington Post* article examined the increase in the number of similar reported incidents and found that the tally has reached over 300 since early 2016. These include bullying like that described above and also the bullying of those who have expressed support for the president.[42] This number is likely understated, as bullying often goes unreported. Furthermore, as the article points out, this statistic doesn't represent the full breadth of everyday bullying, such as the use of pejorative slurs and acts of heightened aggression.

One such incident of heightened aggression was relayed to me in February 2020 by the concerned mother of a bullied child. Her son, a first grader at the time, was told by a classmate boy that he ought to, "Stand in front of a truck, so you'll be run over." This astonishingly violent outburst is alarming and, until recently, was highly unusual for me to hear from young patients in my practice.

In my experience, well-adjusted six-year-olds might say something along the lines of "I don't like you" or "I don't want to play with you" when confronted with the possibility of interacting with children they don't like. The level of aggression in that particular first-grader's statement, however, seems to be increasing among the children I see in my practice. It is also indicative of what can

---

41. Amelia Ferrell Knisely, "Williamson County Schools: Parents upset by racist incidents," *The Tennessean*, March 8, 2019, https://www.tennessean.com/story/news/local/williamson/schools/2019/03/08/williamson-county-schools-racist-incidents-slavery-homework/3067113002/.

42. Hannah Natanson, John Woodrow Cox and Perry Stein, "Trump's words, bullied kids, scarred schools," *Washington Post*, February 13, 2020, https://www.washingtonpost.com/graphics/2020/local/school-bullying-trump-words/.

happen when a young child is surrounded by increasingly hostile and aggressive messages. And unfortunately, our current political climate is riddled with them.

Consider this exchange: At a rally in Florida in March 2018, former vice president Joe Biden said of President Trump, "If we were in high school, I'd take him behind the gym and beat the hell out of him" for the crude comments he has made about women, referring specifically to the lewd remarks featured on the *Access Hollywood* video leaked during the 2016 presidential campaign.[43] In response, President Trump tweeted:

> Crazy Joe Biden is trying to act like a tough guy. Actually, he is weak, both mentally and physically, and yet he threatens me, for the second time, with physical assault. He doesn't know me, but he would go down fast and hard, crying all the way. Don't threaten people Joe![44]

Violence begets violence, whether physical or merely verbal, and neither side of the political aisle is immune to giving in to humanity's baser impulses. Yet this sort of aggression from our former vice president, which is then tacitly condoned and even legitimized when our current president responds in kind, sends a message to our children that this is acceptable behavior from both men.

This is further exacerbated when President Trump continues to lash out at other political opponents and high-profile figures or makes gross generalizations about segments of the population, such as the media or undocumented immigrants. It is easy to focus

---

43. Veronica Stracqualursi, "Biden says he would 'beat the hell' out of Trump if in high school," *CNN.com*, March 21, 2018, https://www.cnn.com/2018/03/21/politics/joe-biden-donald-trump/index.html.

44. @realDonaldTrump, March 22, 2018, https://twitter.com/realDonaldTrump/status/976765417908776963.

on Donald Trump's recent behavior but it is also possible to argue that President Trump is, in many ways, responding to the vitriol directed at him with a more amplified version of the same vitriol. However, his new outbursts are hardly a recent development in his personality.

In 2012, for example, long before he considered making a bid for the presidency in 2016, Trump tweeted about Arianna Huffington, the founder of *The Huffington Post*:

> .@ariannahuff is unattractive both inside and out. I fully understand why her former husband left her for a man- he made a good decision. [45]

Later that same year, he tweeted the following missive towards overweight people:

> I have never seen a thin person drinking Diet Coke. [46]

These hurtful statements may not, on the surface, seem to have anything to do with each other, aside from that they are both insulting. In fact, at first glance these tweets seem to be little more than early exercises in online trolling. But here is where we can start to see a pattern that may indicate that Donald Trump is unconsciously practicing projective identification—or "blame-shifting," as I'm referring to it in this book—whereby he is trying to rid himself of his own intolerable personality traits by shifting them onto others.

---

45. @realDonaldTrump, August 28, 2012, https://twitter.com/realDonaldTrump/status/240462265680289792.

46. @realDonaldTrump, October 14, 2012, https://twitter.com/realDonaldTrump/status/257552283850653696.

When we consider blame shifting while examining those tweets, then we may interpret that Trump may believe he is unattractive, both when it comes to his physical appearance and his character, to those around him. He may also be generally ashamed of his diet, which notoriously consists of fast food, hearty comfort fare, and sparse servings of fresh fruits and vegetables.[47] Yet instead of dealing with those feelings head-on, he has found a more tolerable—to him anyway—approach by declaring that others exhibit these traits instead.

In addition to the psychological damage inflicted upon the direct victim of these attacks, which we discussed in Chapter Two, we must be aware of the indirect consequences of this behavior. When our children learn by imitating those around them, what kind of example does this defense mechanism set for them? Unless we assign this sort of behavior a name, acknowledge it in others, and actively teach our children healthier ways to cope with feelings of insecurity and shame, we will raise a generation whose default defense mechanism is to lash out at others, exactly as we see President Trump doing.

President Trump and His Treatment of Migrant Children

In 2018, photos began circulating of children in cages, revealing the harsh conditions under which unaccompanied minors in detention centers at our southwestern border were held, sparking outrage—rightfully so—and immediate condemnation of the Trump administration. It quickly came to light that those photos had been taken in 2014, three years before Donald Trump

---

47. Ashley Parker, "Donald Trump's Diet: He'll Have Fries With That," *The New York Times*, August 8, 2016, https://www.nytimes.com/2016/08/09/us/politics/donald-trump-diet.html.

assumed office.[48] Nevertheless, they called attention to an ongoing crisis that President Trump has refused to do anything about and, in fact, has made worse.

In recent years, the total number of migrants seeking asylum in the US has surged, from 44,582 in 2012 to 211,794 in 2019.[49] This increase is particularly felt on the country's southern frontier, where migrants from South and Central America are fleeing violence as well as economic and political turmoil. Many are intercepted at the border and placed in detainment facilities while their asylum claims are processed.

It's also worth noting before we get too far into this discussion that there has been a shift in the types of people who have been trying to cross into the United States. In the past, single adult males made up the bulk of unauthorized migrants apprehended at the border; it's now primarily families:

> CBP classifies apprehended unauthorized migrants into single adults, family units (at least one parent/guardian and at least one child), and unaccompanied alien children (UAC). In 2012, single adults made up 90% of apprehended migrants at the Southwest border. In FY2019, however, persons in family units and UAC together accounted for 65% of all apprehended migrants that year. In FY2019, CBP apprehended a record 473,682 persons

48. Lukas Mikelionis, "Former Obama official, liberal activists share 2014 photos from detention facility as swipe at Trump," *Fox News*, May 28, 2018. https://www.foxnews.com/politics/former-obama-official-liberal-activists-share-2014-photos-from-detention-facility-as-swipe-at-trump (accessed March 9, 2020).

49. United States Department of Justice, Executive Office for Immigration Review, *Total Asylum Applications*, January 23, 2020, https://www.justice.gov/eoir/page/file/1106366/download (accessed March 9, 2020).

in family units, exceeding all apprehensions of family unit members from FY2012-FY2018 combined.[50]

However, pursuant to a US court decision in 2016, migrant children and adults are no longer permitted to be detained together, whether or not they arrive at the US border as a family unit.[51] This is a departure from the policy the Obama administration pursued for much of its tenure, which only detained unaccompanied minors in this type of facility. Families were detained as a unit. This court ruling has only slightly hindered the Trump administration in its pursuit of separating family units.[52]

A second contributing factor has been the more stringent "zero tolerance" policy enforced under President Trump, initiated in May 2018. Under this policy, the Department of Justice "prosecuted all adult aliens apprehended crossing the border illegally, with no exception for asylum seekers or those with minor children."[53] The rationale: it would help deter illegal border crossings and lessen the burden on those processing asylum requests. Unfortunately, at no point was thought given to those directly affected by the policy, that is, families detained

50. Audrey Singer and William A. Kandel, *Immigration: Recent Apprehension Trends at the U.S. Southwest Border (R46012)*, Congressional Research Service, November 19, 2019, https://fas.org/sgp/crs/homesec/R46012.pdf (accessed March 9, 2020).

51. Jenny Lisette Flores v. Loretta E. Lynch., No. 15-56434, D.C. No. 2:85-cv-04544-DMG-AGR (U.S. District Court for the Central District of California, 2016), https://cdn.ca9.uscourts.gov/datastore/opinions/2016/07/06/15-56434.pdf (accessed March 9, 2020).

52. "The Flores Settlement and Family Incarceration: A Brief History and Next Steps," Human Rights First, October 2018, https://www.humanrightsfirst.org/sites/default/files/FLORES_SETTLEMENT_AGREEMENT.pdf (accessed March 9, 2020).

53. William A. Kandel, *The Trump Administration's "Zero Tolerance" Immigration Enforcement Policy (R45266)*, Congressional Research Service, February 26, 2019, https://fas.org/sgp/crs/homesec/R45266.pdf (accessed March 9, 2020).

at the border. The system was immediately overwhelmed and unprepared.

Moreover, criminal prosecutions of this sort require separating the adults, who are eligible for prosecution, from their children. Unfortunately, given the speed with which the criminal justice system operates, these separations were often endured for extended periods. And this experience, as you can imagine, can be a source of immeasurable trauma for a child.

While the policy was officially ended via an executive order in June 2018, the Trump administration failed to implement an efficient system for reuniting children with their parents.[54] Families continue to be separated due an inability of the government to effectively communicate current policy and how to carry it out.[55] And for this, the blame lies squarely with the Trump administration.

Reports from personnel on the front lines of the migration crisis lay bare the despair and trauma young children face as a result of these separations. An incident report written by an Office of Refugee Resettlement employee and obtained by the Center for Public Integrity (CPI) included this description: "Minor was separated at the border from his biological mother. Minor was tearful when he arrived and would not speak or engage in conversation with anyone."[56]

---

54. Nila Bala and Arthur Rizer, "Trump's family separation policy never really ended. This is why," *NBC News*, July 1, 2019, https://www.nbcnews.com/think/opinion/trump-s-family-separation-policy-never-really-ended-why-ncna1025376 (accessed March 9, 2020).

55. U.S. Department of Health and Human Services, *Communication and Management Challenges Impeded HHS's Response to the Zero-Tolerance Policy*, by Christi A. Grimm, Office of Inspector General, March 2020, https://oig.hhs.gov/oei/reports/oei-BL-18-00510.pdf (accessed March 9, 2020).

56. Susan Ferriss, "Early Reports Warned Migrant Kids Suffered From Separations. Trump Ramped Up Practice Anyway," Center for Public Integrity, December 16, 2019, https://publicintegrity.org/inequality-poverty-opportunity/immigration/migrant-children-family-separations/ (accessed March 9, 2020).

The Center for Public Integrity (CPI), a journalism-focused nonprofit, also shares similar reports:

> A 10-year-old held in a shelter for two months was found on the floor, crying and holding his hand. "My hand hurts because I got mad about my case and I hit the wall," the boy reportedly said in July 2018. A 12-year-old boy reported "suicidal ideations" after separation from an aunt and a cousin in June 2018, according to a document. In a July 2018 report about a 9-year-old, a case worker wrote the girl "reported that her uncle was murdered by a local gang." [57]

CPI goes on to note that some personnel tried to sound the alarm as early as 2016 about the psychological trauma these conditions inflict upon the youngest victims of this crisis. It cites a report published by a Homeland Security Advisory committee in September 2016, which found:

> Separation can be acutely frightening for children, and can leave children in ad hoc care situations that compromise their safety and well-being. It can also be traumatizing and extremely stressful for the parent who is dealing with the underlying situation but also possible feelings of guilt and worry for their child. This situation poses challenges for normalization.... [58]

DHS's recommendation that "detention or the separation of families for purposes of immigration enforcement or management,

---

57. Ibid.

58. U.S. Immigration and Customs Enforcement, *Report of the DHS Advisory Committee on Family Residential Centers*, DHS Advisory Committee on Family Residential Centers, September 30, 2016, https://www.ice.gov/sites/default/files/documents/Report/2016/ACFRC-sc-16093.pdf (accessed March 9, 2020).

or detention is never in the best interest of children" and that "DHS should discontinue the general use of family detention, reserving it for rare cases," was clearly ignored.[59] A record 69,550 migrant children were held in detention centers in 2019.[60]

Details like these are disturbing. Regardless of policy or politics, innocent children should not be left alone or suffering. While it is admittedly complex, it is unacceptable to perpetuate a situation in which children will inevitably suffer irreparable psychological harm while officials try to figure out a different way to move forward.

Equally disturbing is that President Trump has shown no remorse or regret for these policies, nor does he appear to feel any sense of urgency to remedy the situation. Perhaps rather than asking how we got to this point or why such inhumane practices continue, let's consider why Donald Trump might be committed to continuing these practices. Why would he pursue policies that traumatize thousands of children who are fleeing poverty and dangerous living conditions in their home countries?

The answer may lie in his own upbringing or, more specifically, in the backstory concerning his mother. Mary Ann Macleod was an immigrant who came to the United States in 1930 at the age of eighteen.[61] And while Donald Trump has revealed little about his mother's history, mostly leaving journalists to piece together the details of her story on their own, Mary Ann's story provides an interesting prism through which to view his behavior.

---

59. Ibid.

60. Christopher Sherman, Martha Mendoza, and Garance Burke, "US held record number of migrant children in custody in 2019," *The Associated Press*, November 12, 2019, https://apnews.com/015702afdb4d4fbf85cf5070cd2c6824 (accessed March 9, 2020).

61. Michael Kruse, "The Mystery of Mary Trump," *Politico*, November/December 2017, https://www.politico.com/magazine/story/2017/11/03/mary-macleod-trump-donald-trump-mother-biography-mom-immigrant-scotland-215779 (accessed March 9, 2020).

Mary Ann grew up in Scotland in a small fishing village on the Isle of Lewis called Tong (pronounced "tongue"), populated with homes that were, according to a local historian, "indescribably filthy"—not unlike the conditions that many in South and Central America live in today. Her family lived in a small, cramped house and managed to make ends meet by fishing and crofting, a uniquely Scottish form of tenant farming. The youngest of ten children, Mary Ann spoke Gaelic at home; English, which she learned in school, was her second language.[62] And that, combined with her remote-village roots, unfortunately set her and her neighbors apart from the rest of Scotland and Scottish culture, and not in a positive way.[63]

When Mary Ann arrived in New York in 1930, she stayed with one of her sisters and found employment as a domestic worker.[64] While not much is known about her experiences when she first arrived in New York City, life likely wasn't easy for her. America was suffering the effects of the Great Depression, and work was scarce. It was during this time, however, that she met Fred Trump, who was a rising real estate developer. They married in 1936, and she became a naturalized citizen six years later.[65]

Fortunately, her story has a happy (and wealthy) ending, with her life growing more and more comfortable as Fred, and later

---

62. Ibid.

63. Liz Mair, "Donald Trump's 'Shithole' Roots," *US News*, January 17, 2018, https://www.usnews.com/opinion/thomas-jefferson-street/articles/2018-01-17/donald-trump-should-remember-his-family-came-from-a-shithole-too (accessed March 9, 2020).

64. Michael Kruse, "The Mystery of Mary Trump," *Politico*, November/December 2017, https://www.politico.com/magazine/story/2017/11/03/mary-macleod-trump-donald-trump-mother-biography-mom-immigrant-scotland-215779 (accessed March 9, 2020).

65. Mary Pilon, "Donald Trump's Immigrant Mother," New Yorker, June 24, 2016, https://www.newyorker.com/news/news-desk/donald-trumps-immigrant-mother (accessed March 9, 2020).

Donald, found success in real estate. Nevertheless, we should not gloss over or dismiss where she came from and what she was leaving behind when she traveled to the United States. And while it's true that Donald Trump always speaks highly of his mother—when he speaks of her at all, that is—his reluctance to open up about her background and his very humble Scottish roots strikes me as rather odd. It very well may be that he is embarrassed.

Indeed, his treatment of and his attitude toward immigrant minors on the border, who come from similarly impoverished and filthy living conditions, may indicate a deep-seated shame and deeply buried feeling of disgust. And instead of dealing with that feeling directly, I contend that Donald Trump copes by projecting that onto others. In denigrating those who come from similar circumstances, I believe he is attempting to direct attention away from his own family's history.

This illustrates one type of projective identification, or "blame-shifting." That is, Trump has foisted his shame and sense of disgust onto the children in cages who are waiting to be granted asylum in the United States to erase it from his history and, therefore, from his sense of himself. Those circumstances belong to them, not him. The truth becomes whatever he believes it to be.

CHAPTER FOUR

Learning from Trump:
A Psychoanalyst's Perspective

Peter Alexander, NBC News: What do you say to the Americans who are scared, though? I guess nearly 200 dead, 14,000 who are sick, millions, as you witnessed, who are scared right now. What do you say to Americans who are watching you right now who are scared?

President Trump: I say that you're a terrible reporter. That's what I say. Go ahead.

Alexander: Mr. President—

Trump:—I think that's a very nasty question and I think it's a very bad signal that you're putting out to the American people. The American people are looking for answers and they're looking for hope and you're doing sensationalism and the same with NBC and Comcast. I don't call it Comcast. I call it Concast. Let me just—just—for whom you work. Let me just tell you something. That's really bad reporting and you ought to get back to reporting instead of sensationalism. Let's see if it works. It might and it might not. I happen to feel good about it but who knows? I've been right a lot. Let's see what happens. John.[66]

---

66. https://www.realclearpolitics.com/video/2020/03/20/president_trump_upbraids
_nbcs_peter_alexander_you_should_be_ahamed_of_yourself.html

I n the exchange above, Trump lashes out at an NBC reporter for no clear reason. The question posed by Peter Alexander is what you might call a "softball," something the president could answer easily while reassuring the American public that we would make it through the dark days of the coronavirus pandemic. Instead, Trump called Alexander a nasty person and suggested that he was a con artist. This seems to come out of nowhere, but it is a clear example of Trump shifting blame onto someone else. Trump has often been accused of being mean and of manipulating others, and perhaps at this moment, he was thinking of that. In typical fashion, Trump expelled those feelings by dumping them onto someone else. In this case, the target was Peter Alexander. The exchange is particularly heartless since a colleague at NBC news had died earlier that week due to complications from coronavirus. There is a clear lack of empathy on the part of the president, and the reporter is, understandably, blind-sighted by the interaction. This is a clear example of projective identification.

It is critical to be openminded and to consider different points of view, but sufferers of attachment trauma have difficulty doing just that. Consider how past presidents have gone out of their way to fill their cabinets with people who expressed opinions opposed to those of the commander-in-chief. After he won the presidential election in 1860, Abraham Lincoln appointed men who had been his adversaries in the Republican primaries. Though these men had been vying for his position, when the dust settled, Lincoln valued their talents and believed in their ability to help him lead the country.

Trump may not have appointed political foes to the extent Lincoln did—some adversaries he nominated to various positions include Ben Carson, Chris Christie, and Jim Gilmore—but overall, Trump appears to have surrounded himself with sycophants. And when he's forced to work with people who challenge him—Jeff

Sessions and Anthony Fauci come to mind—Trump keeps them around for optics until they become disposable. When someone in his circle speaks out or shares a divergent opinion, Trump attacks.

Here, I assert that Trump evolved into who he is today in large part because he suffered serious attachment trauma in his childhood which led him to create a persona that would shelter him from his father and shield him as he stampeded through life. Further, his carefully cultivated persona has resonated with a segment of the American public so powerfully that he was elected to the highest office in the land largely based on the cult of personality, which I will explore below. Additionally, I will briefly explain the phenomena known as *attachment, attachment trauma, mentalization*, their relevance to group identity, and how people can begin to heal from attachment trauma and blame shifting.

A Tale of Two Americas

Trump supporters are nothing if not fiercely loyal: as discussed in Chapter Two, the Trump base believes they will be saved from current and future calamity by the president. He has and continues to reassure them that he understands them and their plight and promises that life will get better for them—that, to quote his campaign slogan, he will make America great again. Whether or not he has fulfilled his promise to the base is debatable, but today, America is clearly split between cultural extremities, between the coastal liberals and the vast rural populace. This division has, in some form or another, existed since the creation of cities; it appears that the differences have become downright toxic.

Trump cultivated such a following among conservative, rural, working and middle class, white Americans in large part due to his charisma, and charismatic leaders often fill their arguments with heated emotion rather than sticking to facts. Further, by casting himself as an outsider, he adds heft to his positions by creating the narrative that his ideas are anti-establishment and cultivated with the best interests of the people at heart.

Whether peddling snake oil or manna from heaven, Donald Trump gave the people in middle-America and beyond what they wanted: a full-length feature film starring himself. The faithful continue to believe his message, even when his promises don't add up. Consider what happened when General Motors closed its Lordstown, Ohio, auto plant in March 2019. Trump went on the attack, vilifying the UAW Union and suggesting that it was their fault GE closed the plant:

> Just spoke to Mary Barra, CEO of General Motors about the Lordstown Ohio plant. I am not happy that it is closed when everything else in our Country is BOOMING. I asked her to sell it or do something quickly. She blamed the UAW Union—I don't care, I just want it open![67]

Interestingly, Dave Green, the president of the United Auto Workers, had sent two letters to the president—one in July 2018, another in February 2019—to ask him to help negotiate reopening the plant. Those letters, according to Green, went unanswered.[68] Meanwhile, Trump followed his March 17 tweet with another one suggesting that talks were underway to reopen the plant:

> General Motors and the UAW are going to start "talks" in September/October. Why wait, start them now! I want

67. @RealDonaldTrump 6:27 pm, March 17, 2019 https://twitter.com/realdonaldtrump /status/1107408129619382277?lang=en

68. UAW Local 1112 president writes letter to Trump before State of the Union. Saturday, February 2, 2019, accessed March 12, 2020, https://www.wfmj.com/story/39896004 /uaw-local-1112-president-writes-letter-to-trump-before-state-of-the-union.

jobs to stay in the U.S.A. and want Lordstown (Ohio), in one of the best economies in our history, opened or sold to a company who will open it up fast! Car companies are all coming back to the U.S. So is everyone else. We now have the best Economy in the World, the envy of all. Get that big, beautiful plant in Ohio open now. Close a plant in China or Mexico, where you invested so heavily pre-Trump, but not in the U.S.A. Bring jobs home![69]

The closure of the Lordstown plant was hardly unexpected: GM had announced in November 2018 that it was undertaking a series of cost-saving measures to transform into a more agile and profitable company which included closing plants such as Lordstown. The total restructuring[70] ultimately saved GM $6.6 billion. Trump's tweets seem to ignore the fact that being in the car manufacturing business hasn't been easy recently, and his own tariff policy on imports added significant costs to automakers and their supply chains. But rallying to the cause and creating a new narrative proved to be more compelling to the average American who may not have been familiar with the information surrounding GM's decision to close the plant.

The Trump Show

Now, we must consider why Trump lashes out the way he does, shadowboxing with opponents both real and imaginary. There is a method to Trump's actions. In *Audience of One: Donald Trump,*

---

69. @RealDonaldTrump, 7:37 am, March 18, 2019, https://twitter.com/realdonaldtrump/status/1107607058600349696?lang=en

70. General Motors Press Release. "General Motors Accelerates Transformation," November 26, 2018, accessed March 12, 2020, https://media.gm.com/media/us/en/gm/news.detail.html/content/Pages/news/us/en/2018/nov/1126-gm.html.

Television, and the Fracturing of America, author James Poniewozik asserts that Donald Trump is a:

> TV character president…an attention machine that transmits real-world images from one place to another.…He's a character that wrote itself, a brand mascot that jumped off the cereal box and entered the world, a simulacrum that replaced the thing it represents.[71]

Whether tweeting into the internet or locking horns with journalists, Trump is always on brand and selling a certain image of himself. At the same time, he is shifting an aspect of his personality that he finds unappealing onto those around him. This characteristic that Trump feels he must excise from his psyche seems to stem from his childhood and social background—the Donald Trump who was the son of a poor immigrant mother who came to America as a domestic worker.

And yet, it is his ability to harness this aspect of his personality that enables people to feel close to him, as if he is a neighbor or friend. Trump is hardly an average American living in a split-level ranch in suburbia. However, at least half of Donald Trump's ancestors were poor, let alone middle-class. Somehow, it is this hidden history that helps him connect with ordinary people, despite his preferred Mar-a-lago self, the media-crazed self that is rich, famous, and can boast of having dined with the Queen. Some Trump supporters take his word as near gospel, but the result can be deadly: consider the man who drank fish-tank cleaner after hearing the president tout

---

71. James Poniewozik, *Audience of One: Donald Trump, Television, and the Fracturing of America*, Liveright, 2019, p. xxi-xxiii.

one of the product's ingredients, chloroquine, as a potential cure for coronavirus. [72]

Understanding the Source of Trump's False Self

Despite Trump's outward bravado and boasting of a wonderful childhood, many accounts suggest that his early years were difficult. Trump's father, Fred was a notorious hardnose, while his infirm mother was emotionally unavailable and deferred much of Donald's emotional upbringing to her husband. By many accounts, Fred Trump ruled the roost, and his disciplinarian ways were necessary, given that young Donald proved himself to be a challenging child. Some might have called Donald a bully, but at the end of the day, he had to march to Fred's perfectionist drumbeat.

In his 1993 unauthorized biography of Donald Trump, Harry Hurt III described Fred as a man obsessed with image. Even in 1989 when he was eighty-four, Fred Trump cut an imposing presence:

> He had stooped a few inches below his formerly robust height of six feet. He had lost part of his jaw to bone cancer, his skin dotted with pink blotches, and he wore a reddish brown toupee that always seemed slightly askew. But he still had the strong chiseled features of the cigar store Indians he liked to collect and the bushy Mephistophelian

---

72. Bridget Read, "A Man Drank Fish Tank Cleaner After Hearing Trump's Medical Advice," The Cut, March 24, 2020. https://www.thecut.com/2020/03/man-drank-fish-tank-cleaner-dies-as-trump-touts-chloroquine.html.

eyebrows that had become a Trump trademark….he still displayed the self-promoting sartorial flair that helped him get on the 1950 Best Dressed List along with future President Dwight D. Eisenhower and New York Yankees shortstop Phil Rizzuto. And much to his son's chagrin, he also had the same fiery-tempered, perfectionist spirit that had driven him to become one of the biggest New York real estate developers of the postwar era.[73]

Fred's influence on Donald was legendary. In his first book, *The Art of the Deal*, Donald wrote that Fred taught his son to be tough and efficient. As a child, Donald was sent to military school when he failed to live up to his father's expectations. Eventually, Donald created a persona that was as cutthroat and ruthless as his father desired.

This defensive maneuver is known in the psychoanalytic world as creating a false or idealized self and severe cases could leave the child in a sort of dead zone, lacking in spontaneity and authentic self-expression. Essentially, in these situations, caregivers discourage children to act instinctively. In other words, children will stifle the development of their true personality to please their caregivers. The psychoanalyst D.W. Winnicott (1896-1971) was the first to identify the idea of the false self in 1960.[74] British psychotherapist Adam Phillips clarifies the phenomenon in his 1988 biography of Winnicott, saying the creation of the false self often occurs when children feel they have no other option but to adapt in this manner:

---

73. Harry Hurt III, *Lost Tycoon: The Many Lives of Donald J. Trump,* Echo Point Books & Media, 1993 (reprinted 2016) Kindle Edition. Chapter Three, loc 1078.

74. D.W. Winnicott, "Ego distortion in terms of true and false self". *The Maturational Process and the Facilitating Environment: Studies in the Theory of Emotional Development.* New York: International Universities Press, Inc: 1960, 140–57.

The feelings of real is absent and if there is not too much chaos the ultimate feeling is of futility. The inherent difficulties of life cannot be reached, let alone the satisfactions. If there is not chaos there appears a false self that hides the true self, that complies with demands, that reacts to stimuli, that rids itself of instinctual experience by having them, but that is only playing for time.[75]

I hypothesize that the creation of Donald Trump's false self was the persona imposed upon him by Fred. Donald's early glittery and brash forays in the public sphere are his attempts to construct a new persona, fashioned from pop culture and cues and fantasy. As Poniewozik postulates in *Audience of One*, Trump created his persona based on Hollywood tycoons such Sam Goldwyn, Darryl Zanuck, and Louis B. Mayer in the efforts to transform himself into the ultimate showman, except that the show would be about him. As Poniewozik writes:

Performing himself, though: that he could do. Better to find himself, but a celebrity. Better to find a way to take the job that was handed to him and make it a performance. Better to find a way to convince people that business was a legitimate path to celebrity as entertainment, that making deals was making art (p.14)....Adopting a celebrity persona to speak to an era of narcissism is something that a promotional genius might do. It's also something a narcissist might do. Either way, it's what Donald Trump did. Having failed as a producer, he made himself the production.[76]

---

75. Adam Phillips, *Winnicott*, Harvard University Press, 1988, p. 125.

76. Poniewozik, p 18.

Further, Trump has gone to great lengths to hide or distort his family roots to make his false self appear more plausible, such as the fairy tale about his mother meeting his father. (See Chapter Three for a full examination of Mary Ann Trump.)

Attachment, Attachment Trauma, and Mentalization

Secure attachment with who we are and with other people is key to lifelong happiness and fulfillment. Being able to act and react with kindness, calmness, and empathy are elements of secure attachment, and these traits are important tools when it comes to negotiating difficult situations. Studies show that approximately 60 percent of the adult population is well-equipped with secure attachment coping mechanisms.[77] The remaining 40 percent are insecure, to varying degrees.

Great strides in understanding attachment theory came about in the late 1960s and early '70s, thanks in large part to psychologist Mary Ainsworth and psychoanalyst John Bowlby, who both theorized that babies seek attachment from birth because this ability to go through life with a sense of security is a major motivational driver. That attachment bond, however, does not fuse automatically. Babies need secure bonds and an emotional connection with a primary caregiver that will foster healthy and normal emotional growth. From birth to six weeks of age, babies do not demonstrate attachment to any caregiver. Parents may notice that they can pass their baby around without creating much fuss. By six weeks old, babies begin to demonstrate a preference for primary

77. Kristin Mickelson, , R. C., & Phillip, "Adult attachment in a nationally representative sample." *Journal of Personality and Social Psychology,* 73 (5), December 1997.1092–1106. https://doi.org/10.1037/0022-3514.73.5.1092

and secondary caregivers—those people who are with the baby on a regular basis. At this stage, babies will become anxious if they're separated from their primary caregivers, and this is normal and healthy development. Eventually, the baby will develop multiple attachments with various caregivers.

Ideally, successful attachment happens in a safe environment through exploration. This is a learned process that begins in childhood. Under the watchful but not overly protective securely attached parent or caregiver, children can learn about their new fascinating surroundings at their own pace and rhythm.

Healthy growth and development occur when a baby feels secure attachment. Babies begin to feel safe when they trust their caregiver(s). And when babies and children feel safe, they learn about the concept of a *self* through the eyes of the caregiver. Whether the terrain to be covered is a playpen with colored blocks, a large cardboard box, or a stuffed animal, the baby or toddler who is psychologically secure can encounter, explore, and thrive in his or her world.

Attachment Trauma

When the feeling of safety is in question, usually due to some severe threat, the happy picture of normal development changes. Mary Ainsworth's studies explored how secure or insecure attachment patterns during the early years of a child's life can have profound consequences on that child's mental development in adulthood. In her "strange situation" study, Ainsworth identified three primary types of attachment, and children who exhibited tendencies she coined as ambivalent-insecure and avoidant-insecure had difficulties developing secure and intimate relationships as adults.

Further, physical and psychological safety evaporates in the presence of abuse or neglect. Trust disappears when a caregiver fails to protect a child. Children who are victims of abuse or neglect become filled with despair and are often denied the opportunity to develop their authentic selves. As a result, children in abusive situations will develop alternative personas—the false self described above—in a bid to shield themselves from further abuse by placating their abusers. Abuse and violence against children often result in an attachment trauma, a state akin to the death of the psyche.

Along with causing physical or emotional pain, attachment trauma strips away a person's dignity, devastating to an adult, but crushing for a child. Attachment trauma frequently induces a feeling of shame accompanied by a desire to hide. When this occurs, the victim does not think she or he did something bad, but that he or she *is* bad. This belief stymies the victim's ability to connect with others. Attachment trauma denies or hampers the ability for someone to engage in meaningful long-term relationships by rendering the sufferer incapable or poorly equipped to be empathetic and compassionate. Hence, much is lost in terms of having meaningful connections with other people.[78]

The Key to Mentalization: Attachment

Attachment and mentalizing are inextricably connected. Where there is a secure attachment, the capacity to understand the thoughts and feelings of someone else is possible. In other words, securely attached people can exhibit empathy, which is a component of mentalization.

---

78. Peter Fonagy, Anthony Bateman, "Mechanisms of change in mentalization-based treatment of BPD." *Journal of Clinical Psychology Disorders, 22,* 4-21.

Is it all for naught if children haven't developed secure attachment skills in their youth? No. In fact, the skills for practicing mentalization can be taught to adults. Together, secure attachment and mentalization skills could provide an antidote to projective identification. The link between attachment and mentalizing is clear. Attachment contexts provide the ideal conditions for fostering mentalizing.

Contemporary scholars such as Peter Fonagy and Anthony Bateman have conducted research to discover how mentalization develops in children and how it can be taught to adults. They believe that being able to identify with others helps with developing mentalization. Children who are fortunate enough to be raised in loving and nurturing environments gradually acquire myriad skills including taking on greater responsibilities and facing fears or anxieties that may have at one point seemed unbearable. These children are more likely to develop into confident, empathetic adults than those who suffer from attachment trauma.

A growing body of research suggests a strong connection between mentalization and listening skills. Being able to interpret what someone else is trying to communicate, either verbally or nonverbally, is a skill that appears to be linked to secure attachment.

Mentalizing and non-mentalizing

How can parents and caregivers address instances of projective identification in their children? Mentalization—a conscious action to break unconscious patterns of mental operations—is the key. It is no easy task to learn this in adulthood, but remember, our brains have evolved to adapt and to survive frightening experiences and to process how we interact with those around us.

Consider the following scenario of two brothers; one is a toddler, the other a teething newborn. Jealous of the attention being fawned on the baby, the toddler acts out accordingly—screaming, hitting his baby brother—in essence, throwing the typical toddler tantrum bemoaned by parents since the dawn of humanity. How should Mother respond? Yelling and ignoring the child will not help, but picking up the youngster, soothing him, and reassuring him with love and inclusion will. The fussy child will soon settle down—what was nearly unbearable a moment ago is now bearable, and the toddler goes back to playing. Though the child is verbally unable to express just what is so terrible about the younger sibling, Mother's reassurance provides the child with a dose of confidence that all will be fine.

And clearly, this will not be the only time that the child devolves into a fit of jealousy over the presence of a new sibling, but so long as his parent continues to reassure him in a similar loving manner, eventually the child will realize that there is enough love in his mother's heart for both of them. With patient repetition, the older sibling will learn to transform that aggression towards his younger sibling into more productive channels. These early sensory and positive experiences help the child build a perspective of himself and of others around him.[79]

Adults can learn this, too. Consider an abusive relationship where a husband verbally berates his wife. Relationships built on blame-shifting aren't exactly on solid ground, and the pattern of blame-shifting doesn't evolve overnight. Let's assume that we're observing a couple where the pattern of blame-shifting has been in place for a few years. The husband is petty, selfish, and authoritative. He even hits his wife, yet she refuses to leave. And perhaps

79. Catherine Freeman, "What is Mentalizing? An Overview." *British Journal of Psychotherapy,* 32, 2 (2016) 189-201.

deep down she knows that she deserves better, but at this stage, the emotional pummeling has worn her thin. Her husband's constant abuse has led her to believe that she is flawed and the root source of the blame—it is her fault that she is so awful and that she is beaten by her husband. Accepting the blame has become a survival instinct—to fight may likely result in more abuse.

Now, let's see if we can begin to change this pattern of behavior through mentalization. Arguably, the first course of action would be to encourage the wife to seek shelter elsewhere, but that doesn't solve the problem of the husband's behavior. An objective third party may be necessary to mediate and interpret the husband's actions. I might listen to the husband's complaints and "give back" his rage via my interpretations. This may take weeks or even years of work. But eventually, this man may understand that the abuse he laced into his wife was based on feelings he could not properly express on his own. I've seen cases where men realize that they've turned on their wives out of anger and fear about their own lack of self-worth, and rather than address those normal emotions in a productive manner, they take out their insecurity on their spouses. Feeling vulnerable is a healthy emotion, but people who lack secure attachment don't know how to work through those feelings and so they turn on others.

And, just like the toddler who requires repeated reassurances that he is still loved by his mother, so too will the abusive husband require multiple sessions to realize that fear is natural and that addressing those fears is more productive than shifting them to someone else. The human condition is incomplete without fear, anger, pain, and grief—we cannot deny their existence. Securely attached people recognize these feelings and accept them. Those who have insecure attachments and have developed a false self do not know how to process these feelings and instead see them as bad, and, on some level, believe those feelings must be destroyed.

Although this is not always the outcome of a false self, one method of destruction is to shift them to someone else.

Trump's false self is not something he can cast off like a mask, nor is it a catch-all excuse for projective identification. It is now very much a defining characteristic of his persona. Understanding the origins of his false self helps us understand, in part, the underlying reasons for his behavior.

CHAPTER FIVE

Healing Ourselves and the Planet by Building Mental Resilience

Climate change is no longer some far-off problem. It is happening here. It is happening now.

—Barack Obama[80]

A round the globe, land and ocean temperatures, as well as sea levels, are rising ominously and precipitously—and keeping pace with those spikes are increasing rates of depression, anxiety, and post-traumatic stress. Recent scientific studies have demonstrated a link between global warming and mental health conditions so concerning that new language such as "ecoanxiety," "ecoguilt," and "ecological grief" has sprung up to describe the phenomenon.[81] And now, in the wake of the recent devastating wildfires in California that have burned more land more quickly than any since record keeping began, there seems to be no way to turn away from what is rapidly becoming an existential threat.

What impact, if any, has Donald Trump's presidency had on our ability to deal with the rapidly escalating crisis that is climate change? While some might argue that Trump isn't personally responsible for climate change—and he did not set in motion the

---

80. https://obamawhitehouse.archives.gov/the-press-office/2015/09/01/remarks-president -glacier-conference-anchorage-ak

81. Paolo Cianconi, Sophia Betrò, Luigi Janiri "The Impact of Climate Change on Mental Health: A Systematic Descriptive Review." *Frontiers in Psychiatry.* 2020. 1:74.

situation we're in—his administration's policies and proclamations tell another story.

Sending mixed messages during the early days of his presidency, Trump at times publicly acknowledged that climate change is not a "hoax," even as he memorably refused to believe the 2017 National Climate Assessment produced by U.S. government scientists. The announced withdrawal from the Paris Agreement only months after it had gone into effect under the Obama Administration,[82] along with unprecedented rollbacks of major climate and environmental policies,[83] has not instilled much hope in those Americans who recognize that climate change is real and must be addressed in order to avoid further global catastrophe.

Persevering against Trump's unwillingness to address climate change will take mental resilience. In this chapter, I will explain what mental resilience is and how it can be cultivated. However, before exploring what is meant by this term in the context of this chapter, it is important to determine how people are affected by major environmental changes.

As technology takes more and more of our time as we interact with video games, cell phone, computers, AI devices, and the myriad other things in the pipeline, what is the effect on our interaction with our natural resources? Numerous studies have examined the complex relationship between nature and health, using different frameworks to explore everything from what happens to our brains when we are exposed to, or, alternatively, deprived of, the natural environment, to how our mood or subjective perceptions are either harmed or benefited by the same exposures. Both "Attention Restoration Theory" and "Stress

---

82. https://www.whitehouse.gov/briefings-statements/statement-president-trump-paris-climate-accord/

83. https://www.nytimes.com/interactive/2020/climate/trump-environment-rollbacks.html

Recovery Theory"—both concepts in cognitive psychology developed in the last half-century—posit that time spent in nature or observing nature can have positive effects on various aspects of our mental states ranging from problem-solving and multi-tasking abilities, memory, mood and anxiety disorders, and even immune functioning.[84]

One study hypothesized that a cognitive advantage would be realized through spending time immersed in a natural setting, and showed that for a group of hikers, four days in nature, while simultaneously disconnected from media and technology, increased performance on a creativity and problem-solving task by a full 50 percent.[85] In a similar study, researchers found depressed subjects experienced cognitive (specifically, short-term memory) gains after a walk in nature in a similar way that non-depressed people reported improvements in their thinking, and concluded that interacting with nature may be useful clinically as a supplement to existing treatments for major depressive disorder, which is notoriously tenacious and difficult to treat.[86]

Merely looking at images of natural settings seems to have a powerful effect on health. One study found that "viewing nature scenes prior to a stressor alters autonomic activity in the recovery period." That is, cardiovascular markers like heart rate, systolic, and diastolic blood pressure that were raised intentionally were then lowered faster in the subjects "viewing scenes of nature condition compared to viewing scenes depicting built

84. Ming Kuo,,"How might contact with nature promote human health? Promising mechanisms and a possible central pathway." *Frontiers in Psychology*, 2015. 1093.

85. Ruth Ann Atchley, et al. "Creativity in the wild: improving creative reasoning through immersion in natural settings." PLoS One 7(12): e51474. December 12, 2012.

86. Marc Berman., et al. "Interacting with nature improves cognition and affect for individuals with depression." J Affect Disord 140(3): 300-305. http://selfcontrol.psych.lsa .umich.edu/wp-content/uploads/2013/09/2012_5_Berman_etal_JAD1.pdf

environments."[87] Other studies found that natural scenes could reduce the negative effects of stress and negative mood state, and enhance positive emotions[88], increasing our feelings of "happiness," as subjective as those may be"[89,90]; and, more sweepingly, "Those who are more connected to nature tended to experience more positive affect, vitality, and life satisfaction compared to those less connected to nature."[91]

Revisiting the effects of environmental degradation on the human psyche, one unusual study showed that for a group of individuals who were exercising on a treadmill, not only did viewing pleasant nature scenes improve a set of measures including blood pressure and two psychological measures (self-esteem and mood), but viewing scenes of "threats to the countryside depicted in rural unpleasant scenes" had the greatest negative effect on mood.[92]

Not surprisingly, there is a boatload of research suggesting a relationship between urban and semi-urban living and increases in

87. Daniel Brown, et al. "Viewing nature scenes positively affects recovery of autonomic function following acute-mental stress." Environmental Science & Technology 47(11): 5562-5569. http://selfcontrol.psych.lsa.umich.edu/wp-content/uploads/2013/09/2012_5_Berman_etal_JAD1.pdf

88. Rita Berto, "The role of nature in coping with psycho-physiological stress: a literature review on restorativeness." Behavior Sciences (Basel) 4(4): 394-409. https://www.researchgate.net/publication/268881363_The_Role_of_Nature_in_Coping_with_Psycho-Physiological_Stress_A_Literature_Review_on_Restorativeness

89. John Zelenski, "Happiness and Feeling Connected." Environment and Behavior 46(1): 3-23. https://journals.sagepub.com/doi/abs/10.1177/0013916512451901

90. Colin Capaldi, "The relationship between nature connectedness and happiness: a meta-analysis." Frontiers in Psychology 5: 976. https://www.frontiersin.org/articles/10.3389/fpsyg.2014.00976/full

91. Ibid.

92. Jules Pretty, "The mental and physical health outcomes of green exercise." International Journal of Environmental Health Resources 15(5). October 15, 2005. 319-337. https://pubmed.ncbi.nlm.nih.gov/16416750/

anxiety disorder and depression.[93] Perhaps most alarming, "schizophrenia is strongly increased in people born and raised in cities."[94]

But there is hope. Green space—whether rural, urban, or semi-urban—has been shown to help attenuate stressful life events, providing "a buffer against the negative health impact of stressful life events." Which means the potential positive effects, on both individuals and their communities, are almost boundless. In one study, respondents with a high amount of green space *felt* better, reporting fewer health complaints and reporting better perceived general health.[95] More green space is also linked to less stress as measured through salivary cortisol patterns.[96] Nature can even make us more caring towards others. [97]

Overwhelmingly, the recommendation of health experts is to get out in nature more. But what if the air we are breathing is toxic? Recent research has suggested that "physical aspects of the environment, such as noise and chemical pollutants, may also have a neurobiological impact and influence the risk of depression, especially among genetically susceptible individuals."[98] Air

93. Jolanda Maas, "Morbidity is related to a green living environment." *Journal of Epidemiology and Community Health* 63(12). 2009. 967-973. https://jech.bmj.com/content/63/12/967

94. Florian Lederbogen "City living and urban upbringing affect neural social stress processing in humans." *Nature* June 22, 2011. 498-501. https://www.nature.com/articles/nature10190

95. Agnes van den Berg, "Green space as a buffer between stressful life events and health." Social Science and Medicine, (1982) vol.70,8. February 2010. 1203-1210.

96. C. Ward Thompson, "More green space is linked to less stress in deprived communities: Evidence from salivary cortisol patterns." *Landscape and Urban Planning* 105(3): 221-229.

97. Netta Weinstein, "Can nature make us more caring? Effects of immersion in nature on intrinsic aspirations and generosity." Personality and Social Psychology Bulletin, October 2009. 35(10): 1315-1329. https://pubmed.ncbi.nlm.nih.gov/19657048/

98. Matilda van den Bosch and Andreas Meyer-Lindenberg, "Environmental Exposures and Depression: Biological Mechanisms and Epidemiological Evidence," *Annual Review of Public Health*, April 1, 2019. https://pubmed.ncbi.nlm.nih.gov/30633709/

pollution, in particular, has been shown to affect neurotransmitter functioning, a key disruption in depressive disorders.[99]

As we spend greater and greater amounts of time interacting with screens—in 2019, teens were spending over 7 hours a day on various tech platforms, and that was *not* including when they were doing homework[100]—the opportunities to commune with nature become more and more limited. If we are to increase our time interacting with nature, however, pollutants in the air increase our likelihood of becoming ill. What is the answer? One apparent solution to this quandary calls for cleaning up the air. But, we have a president who claims the U.S. has "the cleanest air in the world in the United States, and it's gotten better since I'm president,"[101] when facts indicate that our air has declined in quality over the last two years (after years of improvement, it should be noted). The quality of our air is a serious problem; a perhaps bigger problem is caused by the fact that we have a president who refuses to deal with air pollution.

Trump has demonstrably flopped on clean air, according to an Associated Press analysis of EPA data[102] which shows a 15 percent increase in the number of high air pollution days in the first two years of the Trump administration as compared with the last four years of the Obama administration. That's a setback from a long-term decline in air pollution under the previous four presidents, whereby emissions of sulfur dioxide—a component of acid rain—fell 88 percent, to below pre-1990 levels. Lead particulate in the air is down 80 percent over the same period, and

---

99. Ali Naureen, "Growing Evidence for the Impact of Air Pollution on Depression," *The Ochner Journal*, Spring 2019, https://www.ncbi.nlm.nih.gov/pmc/articles/PMC6447209/

100. https://www.commonsensemedia.org/Media-use-by-tweens-and-teens-2019-infographic

101. https://apnews.com/a2e7024d43c9409087ec8d5245534092

102. https://apnews.com/d3515b79af1246d08f7978f026c9092b

soot and nitrogen dioxide are down between 34 and 56 percent. Ground-level ozone, which causes smog, is down 22 percent. [103]

A statement released in 2020 by a group of nine leading agencies decried the recent and ongoing assault on our environment:

> Donald Trump's administration has unleashed an unprecedented assault on our environment and the health of our communities. His policies threaten our climate, air, water, public lands, wildlife, and oceans; no amount of his greenwashing can change the simple fact: Donald Trump has been the worst president for our environment in history. Unfortunately, our children will pay the costs of this president's recklessness. Our organizations have repeatedly fought back against these attacks and we will continue to fight to ensure that our kids don't bear the brunt of the Trump administration's anti-environmental agenda. [104]

While a growing chorus of neuroscientists, psychologists, psychiatrists, and researchers in many other fields of study echo the urgent need for us to interact with our outdoor environment in order to be mentally healthy, what we need to do this—clean, breathable air—is becoming less available. According to Martin Hayden, Vice President of Policy and Legislation at Earthjustice, Trump has assaulted the "basic safeguards" we have in place to protect or clean up our water and air. He calls out multiple parties, including "Coal and oil lobbyists installed at the highest levels of government tasked with eviscerating our bedrock environmental laws," and "Secretive

---

103. https://www.politico.com/story/2019/07/08/fact-check-trumps-environmental -claims-1573352

104. https://earthjustice.org/news/press/2020/trump-worst-president-for-environment -in-history

schemes to ensure that the public never gets a chance to hear about or speak out against any of it."[105] Hayden added, "The only power that's restrained these corporate cronies in office is the power of the law."

We have a pretty reasonable idea who the bad actors are in this scenario. But in order to move forward, we also need to explore the initiation of a sustained paradigm shift that involves changing the way we pollute our planet. Who will the good actors be, and what will their good actions be? Only by engaging in an open dialogue about global warming—and facing what Al Gore so many years ago called the "inconvenient truth" about what it will take to save our planet—will we be able to take action to halt the destruction that is causing scientists to make dire predictions about the earth's future.

Because of how egregious the effects of climate change are on our mental health, neurobiologists play an important role in the larger scientific community that is tasked with saving the planet. "The effect of the environment on the pathophysiology of depression is a complex set of interactions between multiple exposures that, alone or more commonly interdependently, affect various structures and functions of the brain." More critically, since depression in our earth's inhabitants weakens their capacity to take action, and is a key factor in the decline of our once-healthy planet, psychologists, psychiatrists, psychoanalysts, and other mental health practitioners are essential to restart the conversation so that the "point of no return" can be averted.

The "Point of No Return"

In 2019, the UN Intergovernmental Panel on Climate Change issued a special report called *Global Warming of 1.5°C* which confirmed:

---

105. Ibid.

that climate change is already affecting people, ecosystems and livelihoods all around the world. It shows that limiting warming to 1.5°C is possible within the laws of chemistry and physics but would require unprecedented transitions in all aspects of society. It finds that there are clear benefits to keeping warming to 1.5°C rather than 2°C or higher. Every bit of warming matters. And it shows that limiting warming to 1.5°C can go hand in hand with achieving other global goals such as the Sustainable Development Agenda. Every year matters and every choice matters. [106]

The language may seem a bit demure on first reading, but considering close to 200 individual countries had to reach consensus on its message, the report's warnings are nothing if not dire and urgent. Many climate scientists believe the earth is moving to a "point of no return" which means that if drastic measures are not taken by 2035, large parts of the earth may be uninhabitable within a matter of decades. If warming exceeds 1.5°C, it is likely that catastrophic climate changes will occur, including the extinction of our own species.

While this is a dire prediction backed by scientific facts, a lot of work is underway across various disciplines that provides some hope. The opportunity to change the course of our future has not disappeared. Dr. Asegun Henry, a mechanical engineer at the Massachusetts Institute of Technology, has isolated the five most practical and effective ways mankind can save ourselves from the impending climate apocalypse. The solution comes down to how we consume energy, specifically "banning air conditioning, replacing cement with new material, storing electricity from power grids, transferring heat through wires like electricity, and

106. https://www.ipcc.ch/site/assets/uploads/sites/2/2019/06/SR15_Full_Report_High _Res.pdf

developing walls for houses that block heat in the summer but let it in in the winter."[107]

How Projective Identification Pushes Us to the "Point of No Return," and How We Can Stop It

Global warming is a manmade problem and so it follows that its solution will be manmade as well. But first, it is useful to look at what role individual psychological states and defense mechanisms have had in leading our society—and our world—to this environmental brink. Psychoanalyst Sally Weintrobe[108] writes about the influence projective identification has on global warming, illustrating how a person who experiences unbearable anxiety—in this case from the idea of the earth's impending dissolution—becomes unable to face the reality of the situation, and in the absence of better coping mechanisms, will seek *any means* by which to cast off that anxiety.

When anxiety is completely intolerable, it is evacuated from one person's internal world through the process of projective identification, meaning someone else ends up experiencing the projection. Where there is a large degree of tolerance of anxiety, thinking and therefore reality testing is possible. Sadly, the option so frequently found in our social discourse is not a nil, but a minimal tolerance of anxiety, which is managed by taking a position of moral superiority in place of knowledge and is followed

107. Jennifer Chu, "MIT's Asegun Henry on 'Grand Thermal Challenges' to Save Humanity from Extinction Due to Climate Change," *Science Tech Daily*, August 16, 2020. https://scitechdaily.com/mits-asegun-henry-on-grand-thermal-challenges-to-save-humanity-from-extinction-due-to-climate-change/

108. Weintrobe's influences include Freud, Klein, Jukka Välimaki and Johannes Lehtonen of Finland, as well as German psychoanalyst Angela Mauss-Hanke.

by the search for who is to be blamed and punished. This seems to be the default position for much of the media and a proportion of the public at large. Witch-hunting and conflict are more exciting and satisfying than the painstaking evaluation of evidence, which requires a capacity to bear uncertainty, ambiguity, and depression. Even in adulthood there is a recurrent pressure for a return to the defensive strategies of early infancy. The preferred response is to treat every new challenge as a repetition of something familiar and already mastered until that proves untenable. Keeping things the same is a major source of our sense of safety. [109]

This description of projective identification seems to fit Trump to a T, since he rails against most everything said unless he or a known follower has said it. Since he is not able to tolerate some of his thoughts and feelings, Donald Trump seems to evacuate anxiety that he can't allow himself to experience. Instead, it is projected onto those who have ever disagreed with him. The "badness" thereafter resides within them; those who he sees as his enemies.

What Projective Identification Looks Like When Aimed at a Society: How Micro-Targeting, Disinformation, and Manipulation of Certain Personality Types Is Affecting Our Mental Health

While Donald Trump is most certainly an independent actor, as we can see from his litany of personal disavowals and declarations, he by no means acts alone. There is a vast public and private machinery that functions in his midst—simultaneously driven by Trump but also driving him. Much of how the Trump

---

109. Sally Weintrobe. *Engaging with Climate Change.* The New Library of Psychoanalysis 'Beyond the Couch' Series Taylor and Francis. Kindle Edition. 148.

administration operates relies on one or more forms of psychological manipulation which can be implemented narrowly or broadly, depending on the goal at hand. Micro-targeting, disinformation, and manipulation of select personality types are a few of the preferred methods Trump and his team use to control the narrative. This is an important consideration for mental health professionals to focus on since the extent to which people are being exposed to micro-targeting, disinformation, and various other types of psychological manipulation has increased exponentially since the last election campaign.

Micro-targeting, "the process of slicing up the electorate into distinct niches and then appealing to them with precisely tailored digital messages," as described in *The Atlantic* by reporter McKay Coppins, has been relied on heavily by the Trump campaign, in the lead ups to both the 2016 and the 2020 presidential elections, but it was also used to great effect in much earlier campaigns, including Barack Obama's run in 2012. The weaponization of micro-targeting is a variation on the use of data that was first used at scale by data scientists at Cambridge Analytica, a now-defunct British political consulting firm. When Steve Bannon joined the Trump campaign, unimaginably large data sets were gleaned from sources including Facebook and, according to Coppins, "Cambridge Analytica worked to develop detailed 'psychographic profiles' for every voter in the U.S., and began experimenting with ways to stoke paranoia and bigotry by exploiting certain personality traits."[110]

The way Americans are being exploited for political gain is quite troublesome. While micro-targeting is used by both parties,

110. McKay Coppins, "The Billion-Dollar Disinformation Campaign to Reelect the President," *The Atlantic*, March 2020. https://www.theatlantic.com/magazine/archive/2020/03/the-2020-disinformation-war/605530/

flooding the internet with false information and conspiracy theories that are meant to toy with people's emotions is a misuse of social media and can be harmful to many people, especially those in fragile mental states. Brad Parscale, for example, who headed up Trump's "Death Star" operation, a sophisticated high-tech facility in Rosslyn, Virginia, is in sync with the kind of campaign his boss wants, one replete with "The race-baiting, the immigrant-bashing, the truth-bending," that disseminates an incredible amount of false information. This type of campaign can be detrimental to vulnerable people who aren't able to differentiate truth from fiction. It can also affect less strictly-partisan voters who are more or less affiliated with either political party, because of the powerful nature of misinformation.

Coppins also details, using his own experience as an example, how Trump's "machine" can influence even a seasoned, disinformation-savvy reporter. In his magazine piece, "The Billion-Dollar Disinformation Campaign to Reelect the President," he describes what happened when he signed up for Trump's social media updates:

> The story that unfurled in my Facebook feed over the next several weeks was, at times, disorienting. There were days when I would watch, live on TV, an impeachment hearing filled with damning testimony about the president's conduct, only to look at my phone later and find a slickly edited video—served up by the Trump campaign—that used out-of-context clips to recast the same testimony as an exoneration. *Wait*, I caught myself wondering more than once, *is* that *what happened today?*
> As I swiped at my phone, a stream of pro-Trump propaganda filled the screen: "That's right, the whistleblower's own lawyer said, 'The coup has started…'" *Swipe*. "Democrats

are doing Putin's bidding…" *Swipe*. "The only message these radical socialists and extremists will understand is a crushing…" *Swipe*. "Only one man can stop this chaos…" *Swipe, swipe, swipe*. [111]

The experience McKay Coppins describes is precisely what happens to people when they are the unsuspecting recipients of projective identification. This defense mechanism allows a person to rid him or herself of some aspect of his or her personality that is intolerable. In the process, this quality is projected onto another person or in some cases, groups of people. The original projector feels temporarily like the "bad" characteristic(s) is gone. The end result is that the first person feels he or she has rid themselves of the attribute or quality and is thereafter, at least temporarily, relieved. In this person's mind, it is a trait that the *other* unwitting person or group exhibits. The receiver of the projection often initially feels stunned. It is as if he or she doesn't know what has happened. Eventually, however, this person may start to *believe* the characteristic(s) belongs to him or her. "Is *that* what happened today?" they may ask themselves, just as Coppins had.

He goes on to report how he soon found himself second-guessing much of what he was reading and seeing in the news. Trump hadn't become more truthful in his view, it was just that it had become that much more difficult to discern the real from the unreal. The strategy was familiar to him from what he'd observed in other illiberal leaders whose particular penchant for "jamming the signals, sowing confusion" had earned a name coined by scholars: "censorship through noise."

---

111. Ibid.

Does Psychoanalysis Have a Role in Mitigating Climate Change?

A number of psychoanalysts have been interested in the effects of the climate on the human psyche starting with Freud and Ferenczi. In his 1915 work "On Transience," Freud considered the ravages of war on the landscape, and I think his observations apply to our current predicament:

> A year later, the war broke out and robbed the world of its beauties. Not only did it destroy the beauty of the landscapes it passed through, and the works of art it touched on its way, but it also broke our pride in the achievements of our culture, our respect for so many thinkers and artists, our hopes for a final overcoming of the differences among peoples and races. The war stained the sublime impartiality of our science, exposed our instincts in their nakedness, and unleashed the evil spirits within us, which we believed had been tamed by the centuries-long education of the noblest of us. It made our fatherland small again and the rest of the world remote to us. It robbed us of so much of what we loved, and showed us the frailty of many things we had thought unchangeable.

Although for Freud and Ferenczi, thinking about our collective impact upon the world was an individual endeavor embarked upon with the analyst and the analysand, the field was in its infancy when they were developing their theories in the early part of the 20th century.

Much later, Harold Searles, perhaps trying to create a bridge between the individual and his or her environment, wrote about the nonhuman environment in his 1960 book, *The Nonhuman Environment in Normal Development and Schizophrenia*. In it, he placed an emphasis on our nonhuman environment, which is constituted by nature (as well as animals and cultural artifacts), and went on to say that it was the next step beyond the intrapsychic and the interpersonal world of the individual.

Others have gone further, perhaps because the state of our planet is deteriorating at a much faster pace than was the case only a few years ago. This new stance was recently illustrated by Donna Orange, an adjunct professor at New York University, who spoke in February at the meetings of the American Psychoanalytic Association. In her presentation, Orange psychoanalyzed our collective reluctance to address climate change, arguing that we all—both oppressor and oppressed; subjugator and subjugated—have been morally numbed by historical injustices, namely colonialism and slavery, and are blocked from acting on climate by our failure to reckon with the past. "What we do not know, really profoundly and extensively and personally know, Freud taught us, we are bound to repeat," Orange said. "Together with the colonialist past we all share, this history of slavery and its ongoing effects, of which we rarely speak, blinds us to the misery that our carbon-and-methane spewing lifestyles are creating in the global south. We are repeating."

The same psychoanalytic methods used to help individuals reckon with their surroundings and past can be used on our collective mindset. "Just as psychoanalytic treatment of shame begins to restore to the mistreated a sense of inclusion in the human community, so can a psychoanalytic sensibility, sensitive to the corrosive and isolating effects of shame, begin to link us all with each other. We can begin to understand that our well-being depends on the well-being of others," says Orange. [112]

---

112. Olivia Goldhill, "Do Therapists Have a Duty to Confront Climate Change Denial?" Quartz, February 21, 2019. https://qz.com/1554808/fighting-climate-change-with-psychoanalysis/

Climate change may sound like a political subject, rather than a psychological or psychoanalytical one. But, as this is a man-made crisis, it inevitably relates to the human psyches that psychoanalysts analyze. Most people go to therapy to address their own personal angst, rather than global crises. Perhaps, though, psychoanalysis could prompt patients to reconsider their focus on therapy as a tool to address their own needs. After all, an unconscious mind perfectly cured by psychoanalysis is of little use without a habitable planet.

If psychoanalysis does take up this challenge, what defense mechanisms will analysts encounter in their patients? Are they the same as those they work with on a regular basis, or are there different ways people defend against the idea of climate change and the insupportable "point of no return"? Some analysts believe there are different ways people protect themselves from the ideas and feelings associated with catastrophic climate change. Sally Weintrobe's work is useful in this regard, as she specifies three defense mechanisms that come into play when people attempt to deal with what might be in store for the planet if drastic measures are not taken. She includes three forms of denial that are specific to this topic: denialism, disavowal, and negation, bringing new and much needed clarity to the subject. I have paraphrased those defenses, as described by Weintrobe, below.

1. **Denialism** involves campaigns of misinformation about climate change, funded by commercial and ideological interests. Denialism seeks to undermine belief in climate science, and authors such as Monbiot (2006) have charted the techniques it uses. Denialism has been termed an industry and doubt is its main product (see Orestes and Conway 2010).

   Cohen (author of States of Denial, 2000) points out in his discussion of Hoggett's essay (chapter 4) that "denialism is expressed in a learned, shared public language; the activities of claim makers and moral entrepreneurs are organized, planned, intentional and—sometimes less obviously—ideological. Hamilton, in Chapter 2, charts the way that "global warming has been made a battleground in the wider culture wars" in the United States. He points out that denialists have "adroitly used the instruments of democratic practice to erode the authority of professional expertise. He means scientific expertise in particular. He observes that one can now predict a person's attitude to global warming if one knows their attitude to same-sex marriage, abortion, and gun control.

2. **Negation** involves saying that something that is, is not. Negation defends against feelings of anxiety and loss and is often resorted to when the first shock of a painful reality makes it too much to bear, for now, all in one go. In a psychoanalytic account this is the first stage of mourning, where a person may begin by saying "it's not true," then angrily accept it is true, and only then start to feel grief and acceptance.

3. **In disavowal** reality is more accepted, but its significance is minimized. In his discussion Cohen writes: "'True denial' requires the special paradox of knowing and not-knowing at the same time." His definition of "true denial" corresponds with the psychoanalytic concept of disavowal. [113]

Healing Ourselves and Our Planet by Building Mental Resilience

I believe we can heal ourselves and work towards saving the planet by developing or strengthening mental resilience—in other words,

---

113. An extract from the Introduction of Sally Weintrobe's *Engaging with Climate Change: Psychoanalytic and Interdisciplinary Perspectives.* New Library of Psychoanalysis Beyond the Couch Series and Routledge: London (2012)

the ability to deal with all types of adverse circumstances including tragedies and disasters of all types, problems in relationships, and difficulties with school or work. People with mental resilience are flexible and can bounce back from struggles in life.

Healing can be achieved by focusing on three general principles. The first one, which is essential, includes our need to elect responsible, truthful leaders who have integrity. In the future, we must have people in the White House who are empathetic and care deeply about all Americans, as well as about saving our environment; people capable of taking responsibility for the serious tasks at hand. These new leaders must have the capacity to accept blame for their own actions without projecting their insecurities onto others. They also must devise an immediate plan of action to halt global warming that follows guidelines developed by scientists. It will be incumbent on them to form new relationships with world leaders who are committed to participating in an immediate, coordinated effort to save our planet. If U.S. participation in the Paris Agreement is salvageable, then that must be our government's first order of business. Merely the expression of interest in healing the planet will speak volumes to our global allies.

If we are to accomplish this task, we must all participate; our participation is only possible if we are each optimally mentally healthy and resilient. This is the second principle. In addition to having mentally strong leaders, we must make sure we take care of ourselves. For those people who are depressed or overly anxious, it is their responsibility to seek help, which is easier to access than ever before. In addition to national hotlines and local clinics that have mental health practitioners who can help, often on a sliding scale basis when needed, therapists from all parts of the country are available for telehealth sessions. If this can't be done by the person in need, family members need to participate in finding mental health services for their loved ones. When the person at risk doesn't have a family to help, community services are available to assist.

In addition to maintaining mental fitness and following sound mental health practices, exposing ourselves to nature, as discussed earlier, helps builds resilience. Those who regularly spend time in our natural environment must be equally willing to engage and welcome those who are unaccustomed to spending time in nature to facilitate a collective desire to save our planet.

The third principle involves the commitment we all should make to help clean up the planet. This goal can be achieved in several ways. Some may choose to donate money to organizations committed to changing the course of global warming, while others may volunteer by giving their time to help these groups. Others who spend time in natural settings can help save our planet by getting involved in projects dedicated to cleaning up our polluted air, oceans, rivers' and streams as well as other programs that are dedicated to removing toxins from our physical environment. Without taking decisive, positive action to keep global warming under 1.5°C in the imminent future, all will be lost. We will be lost.

As Rachel Carson, author of the environmental classic *Silent Spring*, presciently warned so many years ago, "Man's attitude toward nature is today critically important simply because we have now acquired a fateful power to alter and destroy nature. But man is a part of nature, and his war against nature is inevitably a war against himself." [114]

---

114. Rachel Carson. *Silent Spring*. New York: Houghton Mifflin. 1962

CHAPTER SIX

Healing our Relationships with Each Other: Antidotes to Projective Identification

No one cares to speak to an unwilling listener. An arrow never lodges in a stone: often it recoils upon the sender of it.

—St. Jerome, *Letter 52* [c. 342-430]

Time wounds all heels.

—Jane Ace, *GOODMAN ACE, The Fine Art of Hypochondria; or, How Are You?* [1966]

We have forgotten how to converse. Instead, we are pros when it comes to talking at and willfully ignoring each other. Calm, respectful, and informed debate feels like a relic from the past—but it needn't be. Yes, it can be difficult talking to people who adhere to extreme beliefs, but we can re-train ourselves to engage in the thoughtful exchange of ideas.

In this chapter, I will explore the reasons why it is important to engage in thoughtful debate as well as ways to structure meaningful discussions without the exercise turning into a hateful and degrading experience. This sort of activity takes practice, and relies on mentalization, a tool that will be explained in this chapter.

Noted psychoanalyst Dr. Louis Cozolino says we all have an opportunity, especially when working with a therapist, to change the way we see ourselves,a concept I think is powerful for anyone trying to enact positive change:

…states of mind […] can be reflected on and eventually modified. This is accomplished by interweaving the narratives of client and therapist, hopefully leading clients in a more healthful direction. Clients become aware of one or more of the narrative arcs of their life story and then understand that change is possible by creating alternative story lines. As the editing process proceeds, new narrative arcs emerge, as do possibilities to experiment with new ways of thinking, feeling, and acting. [115]

By doing so, he believes, we are editing our lives.

But what, exactly, does editing one's life entail? And even when the very motivation to change is strong, how does one put that laudable idea into practice? If people knew how to change on their own, they would have done it already. I make the case here for why self-help rarely works, and why long-lasting improvement requires support and, sometimes, professional help.

To begin with, it is important to restate what is meant by projective identification since it comes up so frequently and in so many settings. It also occurs in most cultures, and across all socioeconomic classes. In its most basic form, projective identification is a defense mechanism that allows a person to rid him or herself of some aspect of his or her personality that is intolerable. In the process, this quality is projected onto another person. When this occurs, the original projector feels temporarily as though the "bad" characteristic has been shed. The person experiences relief since the undesirable attribute or quality has disappeared, and is thereafter, at least temporarily, comfortable with him or herself.

---

115. Louis J. Cozolino, *The Neuroscience of Psychotherapy: Healing the Social Brain (Third Edition)*, (Norton Series on Interpersonal Neurobiology) (pp. 418-419). W. W. Norton &Co. Kindle Edition.

In this person's mind, the trait has been transferred onto the *other* unwitting person. It has been displaced onto its rightful subject.

The receiver of the projection, on the other hand, will often be caught off guard. He or she may feel stunned and initially doesn't know what has happened. First, the person is unable to defend him or herself. Eventually, however, this person may start to *believe* the characteristic belongs to him or her. In this situation, which can often be extremely tense, the receiver of what has been aimed at them most often takes the blame for someone else's behavior. When this happens, how can the dynamic change between the person who is doing the blame-shifting and the innocent person onto which they have unloaded their own self-loathing?

Instead of the one-person process whereby one person tries to maintain control over another person (or other people, in the case of a group) by shifting blame onto the other, mentalization is a two-minds process in which two people (or groups) have an equal voice. It's a healthy process that relies on active listening in an atmosphere of respect. When it occurs, people feel free to express themselves while allowing others to do the same thing. In this state, a person knows his or her view and *respects* those of another person as well. When mentalization is in play, all viewpoints are valued, and no ideas are judged to be ridiculous or outrageous. Everyone has a voice and is able to express his or her beliefs. In an environment where people mentalize, personal, community, and corporate engagement becomes possible. This does not imply that all ideas are ultimately acted on, or that everyone agrees with everything that is said, instead it means all ideas can be heard without fear of retaliation. This process is important whether people are in school, at work, on a playground, in a family setting, or part of a corporate environment. Respecting that others are entitled to have a different opinion is possible when mentalizing is part of every exchange.

To elaborate on the distinction of these two processes, projective identification poses serious challenges to communication because it can make mentalization difficult or even impossible. In both spoken and unspoken ways, as the dictates of one person stifle the thinking of another, projective identification can ravage not only one's relationships, but also one's sense of self. The recipient of what is foisted upon him or her is left with a sense of false entry, as if he or she has been invaded by another person who has projected unwanted and intolerable aspects of him or herself onto the receiver. This is a one-mind process because the person who takes in the projection is not, at least initially, a willing participant in the exchange. Mentalization, on the other hand, offers hope to anyone who has been on the receiving end of projective identification. The dynamic shift from one state to another begins when projections are "given back" to the person who has cast unacceptable parts of his or her internal world onto another. The process is complex since projective identification is most often unconscious: a person puts into or onto another an undesirable characteristic that is sensed to be unwanted, though it is not necessarily understood as such.

That notwithstanding, the receiver can, in time, when the dynamic is recognized, refuse to accept that which has been imposed on him or her. Whether through looks, gestures, or the spoken word, targets of projection can make it clear that the characteristics that have been attributed to them are *not,* in fact, theirs and instead belong to the person who figuratively accused them of exhibiting something that belongs to him or her.

If the original projector can come to realize the problem resides within, it is possible for a two-minds process to emerge; that evolution can allow for a new way of viewing the self and the other. This shift can set the tone for a new way of relating with people wherein the ideas of both can be considered, as opposed to the previous dynamic, in which the original projector held only one idea in mind. Whereas projective identification involves one person controlling another person or other people, mentalization involves a process where input from all participants is respected.

An Example of Projective Identification and an Antidote: Mentalization as a Way to Heal Differences: J. and Her Mother

J. and her mother, Dr. J., were very close. Each said the other was "my best friend."[116] Two peas in a pod, they said. That closeness began, they concurred, right after the accidental death of J.'s father and Dr. J.'s husband, when J. was seven years old. Everything happened so fast that neither J. nor her mother took any meaningful time to grieve; they just proceeded with their "normal" lives, compressing their family bonds down to just the two of them, rather than the three that were there before, and focusing their attention on each other. That was when they started to dress alike and wear the same haircut. People even told them they sounded similar. J. wanted to be just like mom. And Dr. J. put up no resistance to that wish.

The two were a team, until one day, when J. arrived in my office with a brochure for a 12-week-long summer camp. She was beside herself with excitement. She talked for the whole session about all the new activities she could do at camp, the campers and counselors she'd meet, the songs the campers would learn by heart and sing over and over again, and even the dining hall food and

---

116. This case originally appeared in slightly altered form in *Misogyny, Projective Identification, and Mentalization* by Karyne Messina. (Abingdon, Oxon; New York, NY: Routledge, 2019), 139-41.

"bug juice" they would be served. When the session was over, her mother arrived to pick her up. J. raced to the door to share all of her newly laid plans, only to be met with tears of betrayal. "Why would you ever want to do that? Summer camp is hot and sticky, and the girls aren't nice. I never did that," was Dr. J.'s immediate response. Crestfallen, J. slumped to the floor and cried so much she could hardly catch her breath. As they left, J. still looked distraught. That was our last session before the summer break.

Over the course of the following year, after their months-long vacation, which J. and her mother spent alone in a cottage in rural Vermont, J. seemed to be a different child. There was no longer any bounce in her step. Rather than wanting to play the typically imaginative games she created, J. said she preferred to do her homework. During a session six months after the camp incident, J. was upset about some upcoming, state-wide tests she was scheduled to take a few weeks later, in February. She described feeling that she was being pressured about studying.

Shortly after arriving for the next session, J. told me she thought she hadn't studied enough for her standardized tests and said she felt lazy. She said she hated that part of herself. She then insisted that she had to do her schoolwork and indicated that she knew I wanted her to get to work rather than doing silly things like talking while drawing or painting. Realizing J. was trying to defensively ward off feeling close to me as she had before the camp incident, I tried to wonder with her what she was experiencing to help her become curious about the words she was using and the way she was conveying what she was saying.

"So, let me make sure I understand," I said. "You think I believe you should come here and do homework, so you won't fall behind—because you are *lazy*?"

"More or less," she replied, without hesitating. "You didn't say all of that, but I know you think it."

"Well, let's dig a little deeper. We know for sure who thinks that, without guessing or speculating. But we *don't* know for sure about the other person. We don't know what I think, right?"

J. was silent for a minute or two, and then something occurred to her that seemed to open the door for more inquiry.

"You mean you don't think that?" she said. "I thought that if I thought it, and my mother thought it, then you would think it too."

I asked her if she knew why she might think that.

"I don't really know," she said, a little puzzled by this revelation. "You aren't really like her at all."

That was the day J. turned the corner, so to speak.

After J. "got it," things seemed to shift, both within the four walls of the treatment room as well as out in her larger world. She had become clearer about what she thought and needed, and she seemed to enjoy standing up to her mother by saying, "Who thinks that, you or me?" whenever she thought she was being compared to her mother's way of thinking.

During this time J. also became much more creative and appeared to be on her way to becoming an excellent artist, which was a departure from the constricted way she drew and painted pictures during what she referred to as her "dark days when I was a follower." Now, after the switch was turned on, she explored new artistic techniques, which pleased her. She also talked about wanting to go to an art boarding school for high school, raising the possibility without being afraid of provoking Dr. J.'s anxiety.

To summarize, J. was seriously traumatized by the early death of her father; then she was never able to mourn in a way that would aid in her healing, which further interrupted her development. Dr. J., in lieu of mourning, projected aspects of herself, with all her insecurities and demands for perfection, onto J., who fully identified with them. Blocked in developing her own sense of self, J. eventually transferred her sense of her mother's constricted way of being onto me. Eventually, however, through our work together, she was able to see herself as a separate person, who could mourn, and eventually understand her mother's difficulties without blaming her. She gained the self-awareness and the capacity for self-reflection appropriate for her mid-teens. [117]

J. Changed, but Why? "Redactional Identification" as a Way of Editing One's Story

I believe J. was able to change because she was having a different experience with a new person, someone who patiently sat with her listening while she explored her inner world. She developed a different way of understanding how people think, a new perspective that challenged her old assumption about how all people process information. In a safe environment, her need to return to the same place in her mind she had always turned to when trying to make sense of the world around her dissipated. Metaphorically-speaking, J. was able to explore another way of being in life, one which opened her world, meaning she had a new experience with a safe person who she thought was on her side. This allowed her the freedom to think more creatively in the short term and also to make longer-term plans to pursue things that were different. And she was no longer afraid to voice those preferences to her mother.

J. also spoke much more freely in general, as if she had discovered a new capacity to talk with more spontaneity, something that had disappeared after the camp incident. J. also started to plan more on her own without thinking about what her mother would say or think. What she appeared to bury in her mind after

117. Ibid. 139-141.

she returned from her long and lonely summer in Vermont, was now more accessible to her.

My sense of J. at this new point in our work was that she was able to dance again, twirling and whirling around the room while talking about her future, rather than sitting stiffly at my art table doing her homework. I think she was revising a sense of herself that included the new-found ability to experience internal freedom to feel things more deeply, and to plan for her future. She also wasn't riddled with guilt as she had been after her father's death, and after her mother's near breakdown over her wish to go to camp.

More than "getting rid of" or "putting up with" or "coming to endure" an unwanted part of the self, this new intentional process involves the creation of a new version of an old story. I am calling this newly developed process *redactional identification*, in other words, it's a way of creating a desirable aspect of one's self, learned at least in part from another person, and on some level directed by what psychotherapist C. Fred Alford calls the benevolent "inner other." This "inner other" is an active, knowable and creative part of one's inner being. This concept appears to be related to Cozolino's idea about the importance of narratives and how new neural networks are formed. "… [B]oth the urge to tell a story and our vulnerability to be captivated by one are deeply woven into the structures of our brains," he says. [118]

The capacity for self-editing is an important one for a therapist to nurture, he shows:

[A therapist] can begin by making clients aware of more than one narrative arc of their life's story and then help them

---

118. Louis J. Cozolino, *The Neuroscience of Psychotherapy: Healing the Social Brain, 2nd ed. (Norton Series on Interpersonal Neurobiology)* (New York, NY: W.W. Norton & Company, 2010), 163.

understand that change is possible and offer alternative story lines. As the editing process proceeds, new narrative arcs emerge, as do possibilities to experiment with new ways of thinking, feeling and acting. [...] In essence, therapists hope to teach their clients that they are more than the present story but can also be editors and authors of new stories.[119]

Mentalization Can Emerge When a Different Approach Is Initiated That Involves Change and the Capacity to Be Flexible

In order to illustrate this point, I'll share a story in one of Louis Cozolino's recent books, *Psychotherapy and Neuroscience, 2017*.[120] Cozolino recounts a man once asking him the difference between a rat and a person. Wanting to play along, Cozolino asked for more information. The man said if you have five tunnels and put a piece of cheese at the end of the third tunnel, the rat will find it because of its keen sense of smell and spatial ability. If you set up the same test the next day but move the cheese and put it at the end of the fifth tunnel, the rat will start out by going to the third tunnel to look for the cheese. When it is clear the cheese is no longer there, in the third tunnel, the rat will move on to look for it someplace else. This is because the rat is a realist. On the other hand, a person will keep looking for the cheese in the third tunnel indefinitely, simply because he or she once found it

---

119. Ibid. 171.

120. Louis J. Cozolino, *The Neuroscience of Psychotherapy: Healing the Social Brain*, 3rd *ed.* Norton Series on Interpersonal Neurobiology. W. W. Norton &Company. Kindle Edition. 418-419.

there—at the end of the third tunnel—even though there's no other reason to believe it should be there now.

Adding more information about the reason for this curious phenomenon, the man added that after several generations in the person's world there will be shrines build to pray about the cheese at the end of the third tunnel, gods will be invented to honor the third tunnel and its cheese, and demons will be created to warn against going near the other tunnels. This essentially imaginary, or faith-based, world, and its respective view, will be created because people *want* the cheese to be where they found it the first time. Getting them to look elsewhere is something new and new is frequently not perceived as good. However, beginning to look elsewhere for the cheese can be a game-changing process; trying a new approach when the same old way clearly doesn't work.

Something similar could happen if people who use projective identification as a defense were made aware of their tendency to project onto others the aspects of themselves that they don't like and have trouble tolerating. If they could "take back their projections" perhaps they could come to see that there are other ways of communicating. Shifting blame in order to avoid taking responsibility for one's thoughts and actions never advances the conversation.

Inherent in mentalization, on the other hand, is the idea that people know their own thoughts, beliefs, and feelings while allowing others to have different ones. When mentalizing, people take responsibility for their behavior and are able to discuss differences between and among others in an atmosphere of respect—an approach that could be an antidote to projective identification.

It's almost impossible to consider what is happening in our current political discussion in the run-up to the 2020 Presidential election, without thinking about the role that mentalization could have in our personal and cultural discourse. It is clear that Donald Trump employs projective identification on a regular basis and has since he officially became the President of the United States, in 2017, and assumed the pressures of that high-stakes office. Again and again, he continues to blame others for his wrongdoing.

Here, I'd like to look at a few of the many examples of Donald Trump's attitudes, behaviors, declarations, and assumptions that are particularly emblematic of his tendency to shift blame onto others, while negating, minimalizing, and just plain lying about the reality around him. The topics range from voter fraud and racial injustice, to foreign policy and global warming. Each exhibition of dishonesty has its own peculiarities and dangers, as well as its own remedy. Shining a bright light on them is our only chance of healing ourselves and repairing our ability to respectfully communicate with one another.

Voting

President Trump has repeatedly questioned the integrity of mail-in, or absentee voting, as well as the U.S. Postal Service, which is largely responsible for making sure the ballots arrive securely at their destinations, ready to be counted by local bi-partisan election board officials. Not surprisingly, he has also attacked voters themselves. In April 2020, Trump warned that mail-in voting was not to be trusted, saying:

> Now, mail ballots—they cheat. Okay? People cheat. Mail ballots are a very dangerous thing for this country, because they're cheaters. They go and collect them. They're fraudulent in many cases. You got to vote. And they should have voter ID, by the way. If you want to really do it right, you have voter ID.

These mailed ballots come in. The mailed ballots are corrupt, in my opinion. And they collect them, and they get people to go in and sign them. And then they—they're forgeries in many cases. It's a horrible thing. [121]

The scenario here is a typical "me against them" scenario that Trump revisits time and time again, lashing out at people who do something he doesn't like, or that he believes threatens him somehow—in this case, it is his very re-election that is in the balance—and hoping that by demeaning them, calling them "cheaters," and worse, that they will act differently.

Trump has also on occasion proposed an unusual deterrent to voter fraud, encouraging mail-in voters to *also* cast votes in person, as a way to stress-test the election system. Ironically, following this recommendation, which is illegal, could turn those same voters into the criminals Trump accuses them of being in the first place. [122] Meanwhile, according to the Pew Research Center, the highly publicized attacks on voting by mail coming from the White House have led 52 percent of Americans to believe that "voter fraud has been a problem when it comes to voting by mail in major elections," despite significant evidence to the contrary. [123] A study conducted by the *Washington Post* concluded that 4 out of over 135 million

---

121. Zach Montellaro, "Trump seemingly encourages North Carolina residents to try to vote twice," *Politico*, September 9, 2020, https://www.politico.com/news/2020/09/02/trump-vote-twice-voter-fraud-408007.

122. Montellaro, "Trump seemingly encourages North Carolina residents to try to vote twice."

123. Pew Research Center. (September 6, 2020). *One-in-four Americans think voter fraud has been a major problem with voting by mail, contrary to evidence.* https://www.journalism.org/2020/09/16/legitimacy-of-voting-by-mail-politicized-leaving-americans-divided/pj_2020-09-16_election-knowledge-misinformation_1-03/.

votes were found to be fraudulent in the 2016 presidential election. [124]

The potential ramifications of this denialism cannot be underestimated. In current and future elections, it will take a concerted, continuous, and unified effort for voters to stand up and get their voices heard, rather than be drowned out by bullies.

Black Lives Matter

In 2016, then-San Francisco 49ers quarterback Colin Kaepernick, along with other NFL and professional players, began silently and peacefully protesting systemic racial injustice in the U.S. by kneeling rather than standing while the national anthem was played at the outset of games. This act angered President Trump greatly. He lashed out quickly and forcefully, like any other bully would, using his platform to attack not only the actions he objected to, but the players themselves—and, on one occasion, their mothers—saying things like, "Wouldn't you love to see one of these NFL owners, when somebody disrespects our flag, to say, 'Get that son of a bitch off the field right now. Out! He's fired. He's fired!'" [125, 126] It is no coincidence that he resurrected that particular line—"He's fired!"—even if it was subconscious. It is arguably the catchphrase

124. Benjamin L. Ginsberg, "Republicans have insufficient evidence to call elections 'rigged' and 'fraudulent'," *Washington Post*, September 8, 2020, https://www.washington post.com/opinions/2020/09/08/republicans-have-insufficient-evidence-call-elections -rigged-fraudulent/.

125. Bryan Armen Graham, "Donald Trump blasts NFL anthem protesters: 'Get that son of a bitch off the field'," *Guardian*, September 23, 2017, https://www.theguardian.com /sport/2017/sep/22/donald-trump-nfl-national-anthem-protests.

126. Arnie Stapleton, "Don't talk about mom: NFL players angry over Trump's insult," *AP News*, September 25, 2017, https://apnews.com/e26b0c8327ee4e00931f6fe96def97a0 /Don%27t-talk-about-mom:-NFL-players-angry-over-Trump%27s-insult.

that brought him to national fame on the television reality series *The Apprentice*, one of his oft-repeated claims to glory.

The insults against people of color standing up for their rights has only increased, as the national movement for Black Lives Matter (BLM), which was founded following the shooting of an unarmed 17-year-old African American named Trayvon Martin, has gained strength and visibility. As BLM grows, so do Trump's scattershot attacks against any person or group of people he perceives as being "against" him. In the summer of 2020, when protestors assembled following the police murder of George Floyd and painted Black Lives Matter on 16th Street leading to the White House and across New York's Fifth Avenue, directly in front of Trump Tower, he falsely accused BLM of being a "symbol of hate." [127]

Moreover, he has an equally loud band of supporters who eagerly echo his insults. NFL Hall of Fame Coach Mike Ditka, when asked for his view on the widespread practice of athletes kneeling as a form of protest, said, "If you can't respect our national anthem, get the hell out of the country." [128] Trump has been saying the same for years, using identical tropes about who "belongs" in the U.S. and who doesn't, including in May 2018, when he told Fox News, "You have to stand proudly for the national anthem or you shouldn't be playing, you shouldn't be there. Maybe they shouldn't be in the country." [129]

127. Max Cohen, "Trump: Black Lives Matter is a 'symbol of hate'," *Politico*, July 1, 2020, https://www.politico.com/news/2020/07/01/trump-black-lives-matter-347051.

128. Allen Kim, "Mike Ditka says kneeling athletes should 'get the hell out of the country'" *CNN.com*, July 27, 2020, https://www.cnn.com/2020/07/27/us/mike-ditka-kneel-anthem-trnd/index.html.

129. Scott Gleeson, "Donald Trump vs. NFL players: Tracking president's anthem remarks in war on protests," *USA Today*, May 24, 2018, https://www.usatoday.com/story/sports/nfl/2018/05/24/donald-trump-vs-nfl-players-tracking-anthem-remarks-protest/640055002/.

It's precisely these moments when the president's projective identification is the most apparent—and the most apparently harmful. Instead of meeting a group of human beings in their moment of communal grief, where they are publicly mourning the harm that has come from centuries of oppression in the U.S., and using it as an opportunity to truly make America better, he takes possession of the ball, so to speak, and punts badly—right into the attack zone, forfeiting the game for everyone.

North Korea

Trump knows little about diplomacy, and what he does know, he never seems to be able to use for good—his own, or the country's.

"North Korea best not make any more threats to the United States," he said early on in his presidency. "[Kim Jong-un] has been very threatening beyond a normal state, and as I said, they will be met with fire and fury, and frankly power the likes of which this world has never seen before." [130]

Blustery ballast? Hollow threats? Who is to say what these remarks mean coming from the leader of what has long been considered to be the most powerful country in the world. Though watching the exchanges escalate over time sometimes felt like watching a schoolyard tussle, with Trump calling North Korea's leader "Rocket Man" and a "madman," while Jong-Un mocked Trump as a "mentally deranged U.S. dotard," it is hard to laugh

---

130. Peter Baker and Choe Sang-Hun, "Trump Threatens 'Fire and Fury' Against North Korea if It Endangers U.S.," *The New York Times*, August 8, 2017, https://www.nytimes.com/2017/08/08/world/asia/north-korea-un-sanctions-nuclear-missile-united-nations.html.

off projective identification when it is deployed by two men who have access to the world's largest nuclear arsenals.[131] On the contrary, it's terrifying.

Global warming

Trump's public acknowledgment of global warming vacillates wildly. One day, climate change is a hoax. The next, it's not. He has called it "a serious subject," but also "mythical," and "created by and for the Chinese."[132] What is less confounding—but equally concerning—is the way he talks about scientists and others issuing vocal warnings on the climate, and the work that they do. After 16-year-old climate activist Greta Thunberg became the youngest-ever recipient of *Time* magazine's Person of the Year award, an accolade Trump has on occasion said he deserves, he tweeted, mockingly, that Thunberg "must work on her Anger Management problem, then go to a good old fashioned movie with a friend! Chill Greta, Chill!"[133]

Thunberg is a teenager, over half a century younger than Trump, who has talked openly about being on the autism spectrum, yet proved to be the more mature and self-possessed of the two, when, rather than counter-attacking, she waited until the

131. Matt Stevens, "Trump and Kim Jong-un, and the Names They've Called Each Other," *The New York Times*, March 9, 2018, https://www.nytimes.com/2018/03/09/world/asia/trump-kim-jong-un.html.

132. Helier Cheung, "What does Trump actually believe on climate change?" *BBC News*, January 23, 2020, https://www.bbc.com/news/world-us-canada-51213003.

133. Aaron Rupar, "Trump attacks Greta Thunberg during record-setting Twitter binge," *Vox*, December 12, 2019, https://www.vox.com/2019/12/12/21012511/trump-greta-thunberg-tweet-impeachment.

moment was cooler to put Trump's outburst into perspective. When asked how she would have responded to Trump, she said, "[…] obviously he's not listening to scientists and experts, so why would he listen to me? […] I probably wouldn't have said anything, I wouldn't have wasted my time."[134] She added "I guess of course [the fact that adults including Trump attack me] means something—they are terrified of young people bringing change which they don't want—but that is just proof that we are actually doing something and that they see us as some kind of threat."[135] And it is here that the young woman not only explains perfectly the source of Trump's projective identification, but does it with incredible restraint, steering clear of the retribution or mockery that would have been all too easy to summon.

Under pressure more recently from growing evidence that climate change is real, Trump's claims that he knows better about climate science have reached record pitch. At a public meeting in California, where he had traveled in September 2020 to assess the worst-ever damage to the state from wildfires, Trump had a shocking exchange with Wade Crowfoot, a California Cabinet secretary who emphasized the role of research in policy response to environmental crises. "That science is going to be key," Crowfoot said directly to Trump, "because if we ignore that science and sort of put our head in the sand […] we're not going to succeed together protecting Californians."

Trump responded with typical self-assurance and admonishment, saying, "It'll start getting cooler. You just watch." Crowfoot quickly responded, "I wish science agreed with you," to which Trump said flatly, "Well, I don't think science knows, actually,"

134. Edward Helmore, "Greta Thunberg: 'I wouldn't have wasted my time' speaking to Trump," *Guardian,* December 30, 2019, https://www.theguardian.com/environment/2019/dec/30/greta-thunberg-trump-climate-change-un-summit.

135. Edward Helmore, "Greta Thunberg: 'I wouldn't have wasted my time' speaking to Trump."

and cut the "exchange" short. [136] But, like most conversations with those in the throes of projective identification, this was not an exchange. It was a one-mind deployment of ballast. In any other universe, scientists talk, and the rest of us listen. Not so in the Trump-verse, where he knows what is "right" and he has his own "facts"—what senior staff member Kellyanne Conway infamously called "alternative facts" following Trump's (and his then Press Secretary, Sean Spicer's) insistence that inauguration supporters had shown up in record numbers. (They had—it was clearly visible in video footage—but not quite in the same way Trump had boasted.) [137] While each and every one of these lies is a major problem in and of itself, the overarching assertion that Donald Trump is himself, never to blame for anything—epitomized in his March comments on his role in the coronavirus pandemic's toll in the U.S., which were: "I don't take responsibility at all"—exemplifies the very essence of projective identification. As a hypothesis, I believe he can't tolerate people saying he is responsible for many of the over 200,000 deaths caused by COVID-19, many that he could have prevented if he had taken appropriate action many months ago. Instead he continues to blame the Chinese, politicians from areas of the country that don't overwhelmingly support him, and more recently his own scientific experts, among others, for the pandemic which apparently makes him feel exonerated. The likelihood that he will be held accountable for his inaction in the annals of history is increasing daily, however, and there is some solace in the idea of the record ultimately being set straight.

136. Robert Mackey, "Trump Scoffs at Plea to Take Climate Change Seriously Amid Fires, Mocks Science Instead," *The Intercept,* September 14, 2020, https://theintercept.com /2020/09/14/trump-scoffs-plea-take-climate-change-seriously-amid-wildfires-mocks -science/.

137. Justin Green, "Today's top quote: Kellyanne on 'alternative facts'," *Axios,* January 22, 2017, https://www.axios.com/todays-top-quote-kellyanne-on-alternative-fact s-1513300040-0d8272b0-3610-46d5-98eb-ddca6ae5dba7.html.

CHAPTER SEVEN

Thirteen Ways of Looking at a Pandemic: Trump's Response to Covid-19

I

Among twenty snowy mountains,
The only moving thing
Was the eye of the blackbird.

II

I was of three minds,
Like a tree
In which there are three blackbirds.

III

The blackbird whirled in the autumn winds.
It was a small part of the pantomime.

—Wallace Stevens, "Thirteen Ways of Looking at a
Blackbird" (1915)

Wallace Stevens is considered by many to be among America's greatest twentieth century poets, and "Thirteen Ways of Looking at a Blackbird"[138] is perhaps his most significant work, celebrating the multiple ways in which something as seemingly straightforward as a blackbird can be seen. But Stevens' message is far from simple, as he depicts the blackbird as a symbol for the expanse and complexity of human subjectivity. In other words, the poem is about the different ways

---

138. https://www.poetryfoundation.org/poems/45236/thirteen-ways-of-looking-at-a-blackbird

of seeing and perceiving the world: "I was of three minds," he writes, comfortable in his own openness.

Trump could not approach his world—and his place in it—from a more different perspective. While Trump has a few of Stevens' surface attributes—he is a Republican who is over 6-foot and weighs well over 200 pounds, with experience in business (Stevens sold insurance) and a curiously spiky signature—the legacies Trump and Stevens leave will be strikingly dissimilar. Stevens worked to build common ground through his poetic appreciation of the beauty in and around us, while Trump uses divisive rhetoric to confront and tear down those around him.

How Trump has viewed and handled the Covid-19 pandemic in the U.S. is the perfect case study for how he looks at the world around him and his role within it. His personal and policy responses—sometimes one and the same—are clear examples of the ways that projective identification can be more than just a personality deficit. Left unchecked, it can be a source of confusion, frustration, and loss of trust so extensive that the result is significant pain and suffering; in the midst of a pandemic, these effects come in the form of millions sick, and thousands dead.

The way projective identification manifests as a person in authority deals with a complex, alarming, or unpredictable situation can take numerous forms, from blame-shifting and gaslighting to magical thinking and minimizing. Trump and key members of his administration have engaged in these thought processes since early 2020, when it first became apparent that a novel coronavirus could wreak havoc on America's citizens and economy, not to mention their global standing. And they have given no indication that they will change tack or let up.

Here are thirteen ways Trump looks at the Covid-19 pandemic:

I. It's China's Fault

Blame-shifting does not only happen among individuals. Governments, and their leaders, do it to each other all the time. Covid-19 is the disease caused by the SARS-CoV-2 novel coronavirus that was first identified in Wuhan Province, China, and Trump's insistence on calling it things like the "Chinese virus," the "China virus," "Wu Flu," or "Kung Flu," reveals his penchant for name-calling and bullying. While it may be true that the Covid-19 pandemic did not originate on U.S. soil, once community spread in the U.S. was identified, the responsibility for how the virus was handled lay squarely on the shoulders of American leadership. Alarmingly, the Trump administration's continuous broadcasting of denigrating statements and accusations about Asians has led to a stark increase in anti-Asian harassment and even assault in 2020. [139]

The director of the Centers for Disease Control (CDC) has said it is "absolutely wrong and inappropriate" to call Covid-19 the "Chinese coronavirus." [140] Anthony Fauci, the director of the National Institute of Allergy and Infectious Diseases and lead member of the White House Coronavirus Task Force, is not only a widely respected physician and scientist, he is a deeply empathetic person. "I don't want to embarrass him," he said about Trump. "I don't want to act like a tough guy, like I stood up to the president. I just want to get the facts out. And instead of saying, 'You're wrong,' all you need to do is continually talk

---

139. "Reports of Anti-Asian Assaults, Harassment and Hate Crimes Rise as Coronavirus Spreads," Anti-Defamation League, June 18, 2020. https://www.adl.org/blog/reports-of -anti-asian-assaults-harassment-and-hate-crimes-rise-as-coronavirus-spreads

140. John Haltiwanger, "Dr. Fauci Said He Would Never Call Coronavirus the 'Chinese Virus,' Which Trump Insists on Doing," *Business Insider*, March 23, 2020. https://www .businessinsider.com/fauci-said-he-would-never-call-coronavirus-the-chinese-virus-2020-3

about what the data are and what the evidence is."[141] Fauci is the consummate practitioner of mentalization, taking profound care to listen before he speaks and to make room for expression of opinion contrary to his own. But he also maintains his integrity by avoiding exaggeration, euphemisms, and, of course, outright untruths.

Giving a commencement address in May 2020, Fauci illustrated flawlessly how important mentalization is to growth and healing, when he told the graduating seniors, "I am profoundly aware that graduating during this time and in this virtual way—unable to celebrate in person this important milestone in your lives with your friends, classmates and teachers—is extremely difficult. I deeply empathize with the situation in which you find yourselves."[142]

II. "I don't take any responsibility at all"[143]

Once it became clear that the Covid-19 epidemics in China and Italy had made inroads in the U.S., Trump began shifting blame for any negative outcomes away from himself—a tactic he has never since relinquished. Even as it became clear that death and mortality from Covid-19 in the U.S. was caused by a knotty combination of failures in public health policy and lapses in personal judgment—some of it undeniably preventable—Trump vehemently denied any of it was his fault.

---

141. Ibid.

142. Colin Dwyer, "Anthony Fauci: 'Now Is The Time…To Care Selflessly About One Another." NPR. Aired May 23, 2020. https://www.npr.org/sections/coronavirus-live-updates/2020/05/23/861500804/anthony-fauci-now-is-the-time-to-care-selflessly-about-one-another

143. Caitlin Oprysko, " 'I Don't Take Any Responsibility At All': Trump Deflects Blame for Coronavirus Testing Fumble," Politico, March 13, 2020. https://www.politico.com/news/2020/03/13/trump-coronavirus-testing-128971

In contrast, leaders around the world, faced with the possibility of severe outbreaks, did not mince words when speaking of the seriousness of their situations. South Korean President Moon Jae-in warned of "a grave turning point"[144] in the virus's spread. China's President Xi Jinping has acknowledged "shortcomings" in China's response and said lessons must be learned from the country's "largest public health emergency."

Prime Minister of New Zealand Jacinda Ardern's leadership during the pandemic has been particularly lauded. Researchers point to her style of communication, which she uses to motivate and unify, and "where a delicate blend of language use and intonation conveys *direction, meaning and empathy* (while still pulling no punches)."[145] Ardern herself has explained the role of compassion in her leadership style: "It takes courage and strength to be empathetic, and I'm very proudly an empathetic and compassionate leader. I am trying to chart a different path, and that will attract criticism, but I can only be true to myself and the form of leadership I believe in."[146]

Speaking about her role during the pandemic, Ardern didn't shirk an ounce of responsibility to, or solidarity with, the people of New Zealand, saying, "The worst-case scenario is simply intolerable. It would represent the greatest loss of New Zealanders' lives in our country's history. I will not take that chance. The government will do all it can to protect you. None of us can do this alone."[147]

144. https://www.bbc.com/news/world-asia-51603251

145. Suze Wilson, "Pandemic Leadership: Lessons from New Zealand's Approach to COVID-19," *Leadership Special Issue*, Volume 16, issue 3, June 2020. https://journals.sagepub.com/doi/full/10.1177/1742715020929151

146. https://www.youtube.com/watch?v=ruDJp64prhc

147. Jacinda Ardern, "COVID-19 Alert Level Increased," Speech to the people of New Zealand. March 23, 2020. https://www.beehive.govt.nz/speech/prime-minister-covid-19-alert-level-increased

III. The United States was unprepared, because: Obama

While this next claim may appear to be an objective statement of fact, it is actually a laser-like refocusing of blame onto a single individual. Trump has no shortage of white whales, including TikTok and the U.S. Postal Service, but none so bedeviling as his presidential predecessor, Barack Obama, who he repeatedly accuses of having left him "nothing" with which to fight the coronavirus pandemic. A quick fact-check shows that the Obama Administration left office with intact pandemic response plans—in the form of doorstop-sized published reports—and capabilities—in the form of relatively robustly-staffed and -funded public health agencies. [148]

Unsurprisingly, these claims came to include Joe Biden as the two faced off in the run-up to the 2020 presidential election.

A tweet from September 3, 2020 shows Trump's target-creep:

Sleepy Joe Hiden' was acknowledged by his own people to have done a terrible job on a much easier situation, H1N1 Swine Flu. The OBiden Administration failed badly on this, & now he sits back in his basement and criticizes every move we make on the China Virus. DOING GREAT JOB!

But bullies will be bullies. Not having the ability or opportunity to directly confront the 44th President of the U.S.,

148. Jane Timm, "Fact Check: Trump Falsely Claims Obama Left Him 'Nothing' In the National Stockpile," NBC News, May 6, 2020. https://www.nbcnews.com/politics/donald-trump/fact-check-trump-falsely-claims-obama-left-him-nothing-national-n1201406

Trump so profoundly resented Obama that he is alleged to have hired an actor resembling him to participate in a video in which Trump "ritualistically belittled the first black president and then fired him." [149]

IV. "It's going to disappear. One day it's like a miracle—it will disappear"

This is gaslighting, plain and simple. In June 2020, as cases were surging in new hotspots daily, Trump was still saying this. But rather than "fade away," [150] cases rose. Were people seeing things that weren't there? Was the news coverage of medical personnel and patients not real? Were we starting to think, like the female protagonist who is abused by her husband in the 1920 film *Gaslight*, we were going crazy? In this particular case, it's likely Trump was trying to reassure supporters who might have been on the fence about whether it would be safe to attend a large rally in Tulsa, Oklahoma, where neither social distancing nor face coverings would be required.

When a person in leadership expresses a conviction or a mood, their appointees often blindly parrot and even amplify their sentiments. Echoing Trump's claims of the low level of threat the virus posed were people in his cabinet, including Vice President Mike Pence, who in June falsely stated, "We are flattening the

149. Erica Orden, "In Tell-All Book, Michael Cohen Says Trump Hired a 'Faux-Bama' Before White House Run," CNN. September 6, 2020. https://www.cnn.com/2020/09/05/politics/michael-cohen-book-trump-white-house/index.html

150. Yael Halon, "Trump Tells 'Hannity' Coronavirus is 'Fading Away' Ahead of Controversial Tulsa Rally," Fox News Flash, June 17, 2020. https://www.foxnews.com/media/trump-hannity-coronavirus-fading-away-tulsa-rally

curve," [151] and Trump's son-in-law, Jared Kushner, who in April 2020 enthused about the country beating Covid-19 and the economy and life in general coming "roaring back again" [152] in July. By July, however, the U.S. was clearly still overwhelmed by the virus, dealing with an extended series of outbreaks some called "a second wave," with death tolls setting daily records.

Additionally, the virus has disproportionately attacked people of color across all age groups, even in younger cohorts where age is usually a positive factor in avoiding death. For example, based on data received on June 6, 2020, among those aged 45-54 , Black and Latino death rates were, according to the CDC, at least six times higher than for whites. [153] Some political observers have posited that Black lives are being put on the line to ensure the economic engine of the U.S. doesn't falter. [154] Ultra-conservative pundits even argued that the death tolls weren't so bad when it became clear that more nonwhites were dying than whites.

When Mike Pence was put in charge of the U.S. Coronavirus Task Force in February 2020, many observers noted the bitter irony in the appointment: few politicians have as poor a record on public health as he did at the time. Aside from being a lifelong

151. Linda Qiu, "As Cases Surge, Pence Misleads on Coronavirus Pandemic, Pence Misleads on Coronavirus Pandemic," *The New York Times* June 26, 2020. https://www.nytimes.com/2020/06/26/us/politics/coronavirus-pence-fact-check.html

152. Jake Lahut, "Jared Kushner Said the US Would Be 'Really Rocking Again' by July. 7 States Are Shutting Back Down, and New COVID-19 Cases Have Set Records 6 Times in July's First 10 Days," *Business Insider*, July 10, 2020. https://www.businessinsider.com/kusher-rocking-again-by-july-quote-coronavirus-states-reopening-2020-7

153. Tiffany Ford, et al. "Race Gaps in COVID-19 Deaths Are Even Bigger Than They Appear," Brookings Institution, June 16, 2020. https://www.brookings.edu/blog/up-front/2020/06/16/race-gaps-in-covid-19-deaths-are-even-bigger-than-they-appear/

154. Adam Server, "The Coronavirus Was an Emergency Until Trump Found Out Who Was Dying," *The Atlantic,* May 8, 2020. https://www.theatlantic.com/ideas/archive/2020/05/americas-racial-contract-showing/611389/

advocate of policies denying women reproductive health services, early on in his career he was a vocal apologist for Big Tobacco, downplaying the link between smoking and lung cancer, and as governor of Indiana he enabled the worst outbreak of HIV the state had ever seen by severely cutting public health funding and delaying the establishment of needle exchange programs.[155]

V. "I've always viewed it as very serious"[156]

More gaslighting. *Wait,* someone might have asked themselves upon hearing Trump say this. *I thought it was no big deal. I thought he said only old people get it and kids don't even get symptoms.* And that confused person would be right—which is the power behind people who try to override our better judgment to tell us how to think and what to perceive.

The tenets of public health messaging are quite simple: Build trust. Know your audience. Think long-term.[157] The epidemiologists and infectious disease experts who are on the ground are a good example of how an expert promotes public trust. They are not only trying to figure out how to stop the spread of this virus, but also answer more basic questions like how it works in the body and what are its potential long-term effects. Rather than exaggerate

155. Nicole Wetsman, "Mike Pence, Who Enabled an HIV Outbreak in Indiana, Will Lead US Coronavirus Response," The Verge. February 26, 2020. https://www.theverge.com/2020/2/26/21155286/mike-pence-coronavirus-response-hiv

156. Quint Forgey, "Trump, Who Downplayed Pandemic Threat, Says He 'Always Viewed It As Very Serious,'" Politico, March 17, 2020. https://www.politico.com/news/2020/03/17/trump-shifting-coronavirus-tone-134100

157. Sanya Dosani, Chai Dingari, "The Three Rules of Coronavirus Communication," The New York Times, September 2, 2020. https://www.nytimes.com/2020/09/02/opinion/coronavirus-communication.html?action=click&module=Opinion&pgtype=Homepage

confidence, they tend to sing out a chorus of unpretentious—yet wholly honest—uncertainty. To his credit, Anthony Fauci has humbly but bravely doled out bad news again and again, saying things like, "I think with a combination of good public health measures [...] we will get control of this, whether it's this year or next year. I'm not certain, but I don't really see us eradicating it."

VI. "We've tested more than any other country combined" [158]

Once it was out in the open that the U.S. was facing a major public health emergency, and Trump had changed his tune to openly acknowledge as much, then the more familiar braggadocio Trump has come to be associated with came raining down, fast and furious. In early March 2020, amidst a widespread testing shortage, Trump claimed, "Anybody that needs a test, gets a test. We—they're there. They have the tests. And the tests are beautiful." [159] By May, he was enthusiastically lobbing out inflated numbers about U.S. testing: "This week, the United States will pass 10 million tests conducted—nearly double the number of any other country. We're testing more people per capita than South Korea, the United Kingdom, France, Japan, Sweden, Finland, and many other countries—and, in some cases, combined." [160]

158. Shelfali Luthra, "Trump's Claim the U.S. Tested More Than All Countries Combined is 'Pants on Fire' Wrong," KHN, May 1, 2020. https://khn.org/news/trumps-claim-that-u-s-tested-more-than-all-countries-combined-is-pants-on-fire-wrong/

159. https://www.whitehouse.gov/briefings-statements/remarks-president-trump-tour-centers-disease-control-prevention-atlanta-ga/

160. https://www.whitehouse.gov/briefings-statements/remarks-president-trump-press-briefing-covid-19-testing/

These responses were magical thinking, which is a polite way of saying that Trump was lying, or, if we want to be more generous, knowingly stretching the truth about what level of testing the U.S. had both the capacity for, and the political will to carry out. This is the same person who, during his 2016 campaign, said, "We will honor the American people with the truth, and nothing else."[161]

In reality, the countries that had early, notable success beating back the virus did so through robust testing campaigns the likes of which we have yet to see in the U.S. While abundant testing—in both symptomatic and asymptomatic people—works to control the virus if it is followed by contact tracing and other public health measures, it can also be very alarming, or very sobering, depending on how one looks at it. That's because...

VII. More testing equals more cases

Trump has on several occasions quite openly said that he does not want to bolster testing capabilities in the U.S.—because he didn't want to see more cases recorded.[162] Not only is this a superbly misguided way to approach an infectious disease, but it's also akin to medical malpractice. His approach since the early days of the pandemic has included measures to cloud transparency and with it, the appearance that he is out-of-control, as when he insisted that travelers on a cruise ship—many of them elderly and sick with Covid-19—that had docked in California be kept

---

161. Transcript: Donald Trump at the G.O.P. Convention, *The New York Times*, July 22, 2016. https://www.nytimes.com/2016/07/22/us/politics/trump-transcript-rnc-address.html

162. https://www.factcheck.org/2020/06/trump-falsely-says-covid-19-surge-only-due-to-testing-misleads-on-deaths/

on the ship, saying, "I like the numbers being where they are. I don't need to have the numbers double because of one ship that wasn't our fault." [163]

VIII. Take hydroxychloroquine

The bottom line is that, like anyone who is fundamentally insecure, Trump is on a constant hunt for anything—positive or negative—to be remembered by. Accordingly, he has periodically pushed various treatments, however unsubstantiated, dubious, or downright dangerous, in the hope one of them will be his legacy. While medical experts were sounding alarms about the potential risks for some individuals of taking hydroxychloroquine to either treat or prevent Covid-19, Trump was reporting his experience as an early adopter of the untested drug: "I get a lot of tremendously positive news on the hydroxy," he said, adding, "What do you have to lose?" [164]

But the hydroxy ship had sailed, in some respects. An April White House fact sheet noted that 28 million tablets of hydroxychloroquine had been shipped across the country from the Strategic National Stockpile. [165]

There are worse examples of Trump and various people—for one, the My Pillow CEO who Anderson Cooper called a "snake

163. Morgan McFall-Johnson, "Trump Said He Wants to Keep Grand Princess Cruise Passengers on the Ship so That US Coronavirus Numbers Don't 'Double.' That Strategy Failed in Japan." *Business Insider.* March 6, 2020. https://www.businessinsider.com/trump -keep-passengers-on-grand-princess-cruise-ship-coronavirus-2020-3

164. Annie Karni and Katie Thomas, "Trump Says He's Taking Hydroxychloroquine, Prompting Warning From Health Experts," *The New York Times,* May 18, 2020. https:// www.nytimes.com/2020/05/18/us/politics/trump-hydroxychloroquine-covid-coronavirus.html

165. https://www.whitehouse.gov/briefings-statements/president-donald-j-trump-led -historic-mobilization-combat-coronavirus/

oil salesman"—in his circle promoting dangerous prophylaxes and treatments for Covid-19, including, I'm sorry to say, injecting bleach,[166] and taking oleandrin.[167] They would be laughable if not for the ease with which they seem to result in the Food and Drug Administration weakening their own regulatory standards to push some of them through, their relationship to various financial stakeholders, and most tragically, the people who have hurt themselves by following bad advice.

IX. A vaccine could be ready by Election Day

This is more magical thinking. While the Trump administration enthusiastically peddled the idea of a vaccine being ready before the November election, even giving orders for personnel and health care facilities to be mobilized, the "October Surprise" was never likely to materialize. For a leader to fast-track public health interventions that have life-saving potential is not necessarily a bad thing, but in this case, the results could be deadly. Authorizing the speeding up of trials can lead to skipping safeguards and regular safety protocols. And forcing state health authorities to put in place large scale immunization capabilities before there is an actual vaccine to distribute is arguably a diversion of resources that would be better aimed at known virus mitigation efforts like enhanced testing.

---

166. Katie Rogers, Christine Hauser, et al. "Trump's Suggestion That Disinfectants Could Be Used to Treat Coronavirus Prompts Aggressive Pushback," *The New York Times*, April 24, 2020. https://www.nytimes.com/2020/04/24/us/politics/trump-inject-disinfectant-bleach-coronavirus.html

167. Jonathan Swan, "Trump Eyes New Unproven Coronavirus 'Cure,'" Axios. August 16, 2020. https://www.axios.com/trump-covid-oleandrin-9896f570-6cd8-4919-af3a-65ebad113d41.html

Scared that a rush to approval will jeopardize the public's already wavering confidence in a new vaccine's safety, for the first time in U.S. history, a group of drug companies vowed not to release any vaccine that does not meet the usual rigorous safety and efficacy standards required for new drugs.[168] Some of the damage may already be done, however, as studies have shown that fewer than half of Americans said they would even get a vaccine if it was available, making the road to a Covid-19-free world all the more difficult.

X. The virus is not life-threatening

This is patently false. Trump has even gone as far as saying "99%" of Covid-19 cases are "totally harmless." While the death rate does seem to be around one percent, there is growing evidence that a much larger proportion of Covid-19 survivors suffer significant morbidity. Moreover, a far stretch from being harmless, many patients report a litany of persistent symptoms that range from racing hearts, shortness of breath, achy joints, foggy thinking, and constant fatigue, as well as potentially permanent damage to the heart, lungs, kidneys, and brain.[169] Even an enduring symptom like loss of sense of smell rises above the level of mere annoyance when you realize that living in a home with a gas stove can be fatal if the pilot light goes out and you can't smell the gas leaking.

---

168. Katie Thomas et al."Pharma Companies Plan Joint Pledge on Vaccine Safety," *The New York Times*, September 4, 2020. https://www.nytimes.com/2020/09/04/science /covid-vaccine-pharma-pledge.html?referringSource=articleShare

169. https://www.theatlantic.com/health/archive/2020/09/covid-19-heart-pots-myocarditis/616021/; https://www.theatlantic.com/health/archive/2020/06/covid-19-coronavirus -longterm-symptoms-months/612679/; https://www.sciencemag.org/news/2020/07 /brain-fog-heart-damage-covid-19-s-lingering-problems-alarm-scientists

This is the claim that finally pushed both Facebook and Twitter to enact their first sanctions against Trump.[170]

Related to this minimization is the strange humblebrag, "We now have the lowest fatality rate in the world," which gets thrown around with persistent regularity though it gets less and less believable by the week—particularly for the Black and brown citizens who have Covid-19 mortality rates up to 60 percent higher than whites. This claim, as easily verifiable as it is—it's simply the ratio of people who died to those who have Covid-19—was a persistent favorite of Donald Trump's.

His exaggerations are not always insulting—they are just as often inflated kindnesses or compliments that he doles out as a reflection on himself. "We have the greatest people in the world," he says frequently. They are "incredible people."[171]

In his first pandemic-focused address to the nation on March 11, 2020, Trump stated:

> Our team is the best anywhere in the world. At the very start of the outbreak, we instituted sweeping travel restrictions on China and put in place the first federally mandated quarantine in over 50 years. We declared a public health emergency and issued the highest level of travel warning on other countries as the virus spread its horrible infection. And taking early intense action, we have seen dramatically fewer cases of the virus in the United States than are now present in Europe.[172]

---

170. https://www.npr.org/2020/08/05/899558311/facebook-removes-trump-post-over-false-claim-about-children-and-covid-19

171. https://www.whitehouse.gov/briefings-statements/remarks-president-trump-vice-president-pence-members-coronavirus-task-force-press-briefing-14/

172. https://www.whitehouse.gov/briefings-statements/remarks-president-trump-address-nation/

Sadly, there is much to argue with in these claims, as the U.S.—a country with 4 percent of the world's population—suffers 22 percent of the world's Covid-19 deaths.[173]

XI. "Only 9,000 have died"[174]

Is it possible that when Trump retweeted this statistic, he was confusing the U.S. with its neighbor to the north, Canada, which actually did have 9,000 recorded Covid-19 deaths by September 2020? Sure, but it's unlikely. Canada does have an enviable pandemic record, though: with a population one-tenth the size of the U.S.'s, they have a mortality rate one-twentieth the size. Their strategy might be characterized in this way: cautious, clear, and candid.

This is merely a variation on the regular minimization Trump engages in when it comes to the severity of Covid-19, but it is an important one because it reveals an important source of misinformation that guides an alarmingly large swath of thinking—on both the right and the left—by the American people: the conspiracy theory.

Trump embraces fringe theories about Covid-19 with the same enthusiasm he promotes fringe treatments. By late August, in an epic night of tweeting 88 times, Trump retweeted a story about Covid-19 deaths asserting that the real death toll from the coronavirus is only around 9,000—not more than 20 times that

173. Nicholas Kristof, " 'I Keep My Promises,' Trump Said. Let's Check." *The New York Times.* September 5, 2020. https://www.nytimes.com/2020/09/05/opinion/sunday/trump-promises-check.html?action=click&module=Opinion&pgtype=Homepage

174. Peter Baker, "Trump Embraces Fringe Theories on Protests and the Coronavirus," *The New York Times,* September 16, 2020. https://www.nytimes.com/2020/08/30/us/politics/trump-protests-violence-coronavirus.html?action=click&module=Top%20Stories&pgtype=Homepage

amount—because the others who died also had other health issues and most were of an advanced age.[175] This is a QAnon conspiracy theory that, following Trump's tweets, was quickly echoed in the U.S. House of Representatives by GOP senators.

Conspiracy hawks know that amplification is key to solidifying belief in unfounded ideas. The more frequently we hear something, whether it crosses our social media feeds or the lips of a friend, the more challenging it is to see it as not true.

The point is to distract from the reality and severity of the situation. The numbers are truly shocking. By Election Day, the U.S. will have over 200,000 deaths. That is one in 1,600 Americans. Imagine a sinkhole opening up in the middle of Salt Lake City, and every resident just *disappearing* into it, never to be seen again. The book *The New York Times* published after 9/11[176] to memorialize the over 2,750 people killed by that terrorist attack runs 555 pages. A similar book, memorializing U.S. Covid-19 deaths would be over *forty thousand* pages long.

What's more, because of the way these deaths are counted, this number is likely an undercount of true Covid-19 deaths.[177]

XII. Schools must open, sports must be played, rallies must be held

Remember the analogy questions on the standardized tests you took growing up? "Dog is to cat as puppy is to kitten," for example. Here's another:

175. https://www.nytimes.com/2020/08/30/us/politics/trump-protests-violence-corona virus.html?action=click&module=Top%20Stories&pgtype=Homepage

176. *The New York Times* Staff, *Portraits: 9/11/01: The Collected "Portraits of Grief" from The New York Times*. New York, NY: Times Books, Henry Holt & Co. 2002.

177. https://fivethirtyeight.com/features/coronavirus-deaths/

Build the Wall : Immigration :: Send Kids to School :
Coronavirus.

A "solution" and a problem. In July, Trump announced, "So
what we want to do is we want to get our schools open. We want
to get them open quickly, beautifully, in the fall." [178] Like any other
pronouncement made by a politician, this type of broad-brush
plan that is unsupported by efficacy data, often wends its way
into policies. What plans for opening schools and playing sports
lack in evidence is made up for in the sheer enthusiasm people
have for them. Much like building a physical wall, holding rallies
and other large gatherings offer clear optics, first and foremost.
But their longer-term effects are not fully known, and their general
soundness is questionable. Just as spending millions on a metal
fence has not led to decreases in unauthorized immigration, [179]
it's unclear who or what living in dorms and attending class in
person and playing football and assembling in crowds—whether
for political rallies or Big 10 games—actually serves. The only
thing that is clear is that the consequences of these choices is
unknown and potentially dangerous.

While there was no counterfactual at the time that Trump
called for classroom teaching to start up, by mid-Fall 2020, it
was clear that many colleges and universities that had opened
dorms and held in-person classes experienced quite severe campus outbreaks. [180] Not to mention the Greek life on campus that

178. https://www.whitehouse.gov/briefings-statements/remarks-president-trump-safely
-reopening-americas-schools/

179. Adam Isacson, "The U.S. Government's 2018 Border Data Clearly Shows Why the
Trump Administration is on the Wrong Track," WOLA, November 9, 2018. https://www
.wola.org/analysis/us-government-2018-border-data-trump-immigration-asylum-policy/

180. IHE Staff, "COVID-19 Roundup: Colleges Struggle to Control Outbreaks," Inside
Higher Ed. August 31, 2020. https://www.insidehighered.com/news/2020/08/31/covid
-19-roundup-cases-surge-new-restrictions-emerge

proceeded with business as usual, meaning crowded basement parties were held and beer pong was played. Because: young adults. But also because, as sociologist Zeynep Tufekci has written, one of the less obvious, or "latent" functions of the in-person college experience is socialization.[181] Not taking into consideration what might happen once a sweeping recommendation is issued, not thinking beyond the immediate curb-appeal of having things look a certain way, with fans and students and sign-waving supporters in seats, is also a symptom of the blinkered vision that people with projective identification display.

XIII. Masks are useless, Actually, masks look cool: wear a mask. Scratch that—no mask necessary.

This final way of looking at Covid-19 is an interesting one because it defies logic. Trump is a self-described germaphobe who acknowledged decades ago on Howard Stern's radio show that he suffers from obsessive-compulsive disorder. Before he was president, he was notorious for refusing to shake hands, calling the practice "barbaric,"[182] and saying, "I happen to be a clean hands freak. I feel much better after I thoroughly wash my hands, which I do as much as possible."

It's important to say that people diagnosed with mysophobia—the psychological term for an "extreme or irrational fear of dirt or contamination"—should never be dismissed. It is a mental health problem that can be a terrible burden on its sufferers, who

---

181. Zeynep Tufekci, "The Pandemic Is No Excuse to Surveil Students," *The Atlantic*, September 4, 2020. https://www.theatlantic.com/technology/archive/2020/09/pandemic -no-excuse-colleges-surveil-students/616015/

182. Dan Amira, "Does Donald Trump Have a Flesh-Pressing Problem?" *New York Magazine*, February 25, 2011. https://nymag.com/intelligencer/2011/02/does_donald _trump_have_a_glad-.html

often experience interruptions in their daily living due to isolation, avoidance, and compulsive behavior.

So why has Trump flip-flopped on wearing a mask—a fairly simple thing to do that has evidence-based results? And why have the administration's recommendations on masks and social distancing—which actually includes encouraging elbow bumps instead of the handshaking which the president now seems to enthusiastically engage in—never squared with Trump's personal attitudes or behaviors? What to make of this? What kind of mental contortionism does he need to do to get to this position on masks?

The answers to these questions might have to do with ego. One of the few times Trump did wear a mask after long resisting guidance from the CDC for all Americans to do so, he compared his appearance to a fictional character known for upholding law and order in the American West, saying, "I sort of liked the way I looked. OK. I thought it was OK. It was a dark black mask, and I thought it looked OK. [...] It looked like the Lone Ranger."[183]

Trump has also mocked Joe Biden for wearing a mask, asking his supporters if they know "a man that likes a mask as much" as Biden. "It gives him a feeling of security. If I was a psychiatrist, I'd say this guy has some big issues," he went on to say at a rally in September.[184] Only the day before, however, he had lambasted Speaker of the House Nancy Pelosi for *not* wearing a mask during a hairstyling appointment, tweeting:

Crazy Nancy Pelosi is being decimated for having a beauty parlor opened, when all others are closed, and for not

183. Aamer Madhani, Darlene Superville, "Trump Says He Looks Like the Lone Ranger in a Mask and Likes It," Associated Press. July 1, 2020. https://apnews.com/1e44ece4bdb 023fbcd7de93def02c475

184. Paul LeBlanc, "Trump Mocks Biden for Wearing Mask: 'Did You Ever See a Man That Likes a Mask as Much as Him?'" CNN, September 3, 2020. https://www.cnn .com/2020/09/03/politics/trump-biden-coronavirus-mask/index.html

wearing a Mask - despite constantly lecturing everyone else. We will almost certainly take back the House, and send Nancy packing![185]

By late summer, Trump was back to going without a mask. At the Republican National Convention held on the lawn of the White House in August 2020, over 1500 guests sat side by side, virtually all of them maskless, as Trump minimized the extent of infection rates across the U.S., declaring his administration's Covid-19 response a fait accompli of successful disease eradication.[186, 187]

Anthony Fauci, in contrast, approaches the public's mixed record on mask-wearing with empathy, making a point to honestly acknowledge early cross-talk on masks: "We have to admit it, that mixed message in the beginning, even though it was well-meant to allow masks to be available for health workers, that was detrimental in getting the message across," he said.[188]

What results is once again confusion, with even those who want to do the right thing and stop the spread of Covid-19 unable to act with confidence. Projective identification doesn't just hurt feelings, it maims and kills, and sometimes on the order

185. Darragh Roche, "Trump Scolds Pelosi Over Hair Salon Trip After 'Lecturing Everyone' About Masks," Newsweek, September 2, 2020. https://www.newsweek.com /trump-pelosi-hair-salon-lecturing-everyone-masks-1529163

186. Linda Qiu and Sherly Gay Stolberg, "For Trump, G.O.P. Created an Alternative America Beyond COVID-19," The New York Times, August 28, 2020. https://www .nytimes.com/2020/08/28/us/politics/trump-coronavirus-fact-check.html

187. David Jackson, "Donald Trump Goes Maskless in Kenosha, and Urges Others to Do So Despite COVID-19 Order," USA Today, September 1, 2020. https://www.usatoday. com/story/news/politics/2020/09/01/donald-trump-no-mask-kenosha-despite-covid-19 -spread-wisconsin/5682906002/

188. Emma Betuel, "Fauci Dispatch : 4 Fauci Quotes Sum up What You Need to Know About COVID-19 This Week." Inverse. August 26, 2020. https://www.inverse.com /mind-body/4-fauci-quotes-explained

of hundreds of thousands of people. The consequences of this messaging and contradictory action will be borne out for decades to come.

In his nomination speech at the July 2016 GOP convention, Trump himself identified the magnitude of a president's responsibility, saying, in hindsight, what comes across as almost farcical, "The most basic duty of government is to defend the lives of its own citizens. Any government that fails to do so is a government unworthy to lead."[189]

These thirteen ways of looking at a pandemic focus on the litany of obfuscations and outright rejections of science Trump doles out time and time again, and the chaos that has ensued. Are all these stances and reactions to crisis rooted in defense mechanisms? Is Trump a sadist, as some have claimed, who enjoys unleashing chaos and pain on others? Many defense mechanisms are subconscious, barely intelligible to the person who is acting, but anything to do with Covid-19 and the president is acted out on center stage.

His words are powerful, just as the optics of his policies are powerful. But we mustn't forget that we have power, too.

In "Thirteen Ways of Looking at a Blackbird," Stevens uses the twelfth stanza to emphasize the blackbird's—and by extension, his own—consistency.

XII

The river is moving.
The blackbird must be flying.
To that I would add:
And Trump must be lying.

---

189. Transcript. https://www.nytimes.com/2016/07/22/us/politics/trump-transcript-rnc-address.html

CHAPTER EIGHT

Transformative Conversations:
A Way Ahead

E nergy is neither created nor destroyed, as Albert Einstein's
most influential theory proved, but rather is *transformed*
from one state to another. The same principle applies to
aggression which is present in human beings almost from the
beginning of life; sometimes it is turned inward and sometimes
it is turned outward, but it never simply evaporates or disappears.
Whether we are born with aggressive tendencies or whether it is
a temperament that we develop over the course of our lives, aggression is a distinctly universal human trait. At different times, it
might be challenged, ignored, or "swept under the rug," metaphor-
ically speaking, but there it remains—it will never just go away.

I'd like to discuss the dynamics of aggression within a particular
family over a series of years, using the example of a setting that
is familiar to every American: the annual Thanksgiving Dinner.

Warm Anticipation

Lyle and Kelly have been together for six years and engaged for
two of those. They were looking forward to their trip to Newport
for Thanksgiving. Kelly grew up in Rhode Island and loved to visit
on holidays. Lyle was from the Midwest but loved Kelly's family.
Her brothers, who all went to Ivy League schools, as had Lyle
and Kelly, were bright, fun-loving, and always ready to engage in

stimulating conversations. Other relatives in her fiancé's extended family were great conversationalists, too. Lyle particularly liked talking to Kelly's uncles, real salt-of-the earth types. While the whole family had done well financially, several of these men made money the hard way by working their way up from stock boys to CEOs. That generation of brothers had moved away from Rhode Island, to various parts of the country. They were politically conservative and called themselves "Reagan Republicans," that is, all of them except Kelly's father, who was a card-carrying Democrat. Since the time when he had first spent time with Kelly's family, Lyle had loved the family's ability to discuss various divergent political views openly, and with respect for one another.

The Quintessential Thanksgiving

For many years, the celebration unfolded in a pleasant, if predictable way. As guests gathered for Thanksgiving dinner, there was usually talk about the turkey, whether it was moist or dry or if deep-frying had once and for all knocked roasting "out of the park." There were comments about the "wonderful" or "not-so-great" stuffing, with some hinting that they preferred Aunt Jessie's version with the chestnuts. And there was the inevitable recollection of desserts from previous years, and shared hopes that the pie would be made from fresh pumpkin this year.

These light-hearted discussions were the backdrop during holiday events for years, as people gathered from points afar, from California to New York and all areas in between. Younger generations might have talked about their college experiences, with or without adults around, and new parents often boasted about what was happening at Evan's or Ellie's preschool. The most contentious conversations involved wagering on how tipsy Aunt

Grace might get this year. Religious topics were generally avoided at these gatherings, in case people of different faiths might be at odds with each other's beliefs. Everyone ought to feel welcome and appreciated, was the overarching tenor of the day. Other than that, though, as long as topics were age-appropriate and above board for all attendees, most people usually had a good time. That is, unless Uncle Pete got drunk and accused the host of having over-served him or some other accusation that often accompanies being inebriated.

Often people brought guests or invited others who had no place to go. No matter how people celebrated Thanksgiving there was generally a sense of well-being, thankfulness for the time spent with family and friends, or at least an appreciation for the time they had off from work.

"Please Join Us, *and*..." The Invitation Takes a Turn

After the 2016 presidential election, what had once been straight-forward extensions of a warm welcome to spend a memorable day together with extended family and friends had changed. For people like Kelly and Lyle, who had always loved to get together for holidays, the new type of invitation, whether sent electron-ically, through the postal service, or by word of mouth, seemed like it could put a damper on their family celebration. Now, the Thanksgiving dinner invite or evite they so looked forward to each year included additional information, reading:

> "Please join us for our traditional Feast of Thanksgiving
> with good wine, Elizabeth's gourmet cuisine and stimu-
> lating conversation. This year we have one request. Since
> our country is currently so divided about politics, we are

asking our guests not to discuss the current administration or any of their political views since such topics are causing a great deal of acrimony among family members these days.

We can't wait to see all of you.

Warm regards,
Charles and Elizabeth"

Okay, Lyle and Kelly said to one another, not sure what to expect. And they were far from alone.

Whether stated formally or not, the prohibition against talking about politics has spread throughout America in the years since Donald Trump's presidency began. The days of reminiscing about family picnics, sailing to the Cape, or whispers about Aunt Grace's tipsiness have faded into near oblivion, replaced by vitriolic and bitter arguments between the pro-Trump and anti-Trump factions within families. Hence, the guidelines about conversations in the 2019 invitation.

While many guests I imagine have abided by the request of their hosts to keep politics out of family conversations during the holidays, what has happened instead is that thoughts and opinions about happenings in Washington, D.C. have been swept under the rug. One has to wonder about the implications of this type of censorship. Is it actually helpful to limit what people can talk about at family events? What happens to pent up feelings that can't be expressed? What messages are we giving to our children about keeping thoughts and opinions to ourselves because different ideas might not be well received by others, or worse yet, may cause major rifts in families?

In spite of differing political viewpoints, I believe it is possible to share opinions while maintaining an atmosphere of trust and respect. Here's an example of how such a conversation might be initiated and then conducted, along with ways of redirecting potential acrimonious undertones.

The Invitation of the Future

As with much else in life, managing expectations and modeling healthy communication is key to rewarding and harmonious intellectual exchange. An invitation to listen, as opposed to ignoring or combatting views that differ from our own is the first step to a positive and memorable celebration:

> "Please join us for our traditional Feast of Thanksgiving with good wine, Elizabeth's gourmet cuisine and stimulating conversation. This year we invite you to discuss current events and political developments in your part of the world, as well as your views about our current leaders. We ask that you listen to the views of others in a respectful way. We do not expect our guests to agree on controversial topics but request that we all appreciate the rights of others to have differing views.

> We hope you will be able to join us.

> Warm regards,
> Charles and Elizabeth"

Thanksgiving Beyond 2020: A Proposed Dialogue

Although politics had been a forbidden topic in the Jenkins home since 2017, Lyle and Kelly sincerely hope that invitations in future years will be different. They envision, as suggested above, that people will be invited to talk about various topics, including politics. The only rule that will be required is to respect the opinions of others, even when they differ quite dramatically from one's own views.

For Lyle and Kelly, as well as the other invitees, future holiday events might look like this exchange:

Uncle John: "Well that was an interesting invitation you sent out, brother. I was kind of surprised since you insisted that we weren't supposed talk about politics for the last several years. Don't get me wrong—I understood the reasoning behind it. People in my office practically throw things at each other because they're on different sides of political issues. But, here, among my family where I can usually speak freely, it was hard."

Uncle Charles: "John, I get it. Silencing everyone was the last thing I wanted to do, but it got so contentious when we started to talk about Trump that it seemed to Elizabeth and me it was better to just not talk about politics at all. In our synagogue we had discussions about it and there seemed to be the consensus that it was better to spend time with relatives and friends being thankful for what we all have rather than to get in acrimonious discussions about Trump. Our neighbors next door, the Petersons, said they had the same discussions at their church. They said they reached the same conclusion: Talk about children and grandchildren as well as about successes and achievements, rather than the ups and downs of Donald Trump. Upbeat subjects just seem more conducive to family health.

This year, though, I read a book that really inspired me. It was about dealing with conflict rather than running away from it. It emphasized the benefits of facing conflict head on and taking the time to explain and understand where people are coming from.

Based on what I read, I decided that it would be better for us to talk about differences rather than bury them, too. Long after Trump is gone, the tensions that have developed between people on both sides of the aisle won't go away without talking about them. The memories of tense Thanksgiving dinners that have been politely buried and never looked at again won't just disappear.

So, I'd like to say to you, my family and friends: feel free to speak about your views, whatever they may be. The only rule Elizabeth and I have is that you maintain respect for others who have different views than yours.

I'll take the risk by starting. I think the Trump Administration is a disaster. Having worked in Washington for so many years, I've seen all kinds of presidents come and go. I felt like I'd seen it all. There have been many views that I've disagreed with, but I've never seen such hatred, even in the Nixon Administration. Richard Nixon was problematic as a president in many ways, we all know that, but he didn't think he was king. Ultimately, on some level, he knew there were boundaries he couldn't cross. This guy thinks he can do anything. He really seems to believe the First Amendment gives him the right to say whatever he wants, whether it's true or not, bar nothing. Well, I've said my piece, that's enough for now."

<u>Aunt Julie, Charles's sister, spoke next</u>: "This is hard, Charles. We grew up in a very Republican family. While I do respect your views, they're a little hard to hear. However, more important than my reaction to the content of what you were saying, I am so thankful that you have given us all the opportunity to voice our own opinions without fear of reprisal. I'll share my opinion and then maybe we can talk about these differences in a calm and respectful manner.

I am not a Trump Republican now, but I will probably vote for him again because I think he cares about the average citizen. He wants to bring our troops back from the Middle East, he wants us to be able to produce our own natural resources without depending on countries like Iran, Saudi Arabia, and all of the other places that hold us hostage because of their oil. He's made people in our community feel heard—I feel like I'm part of something bigger than myself. I was listening to a TV station I don't usually listen to, and they were saying something about the Trump base. The commentator said we are not educated people. That sounded so negative and it's not accurate, at least not in my circle of friends. All of us have college degrees and in some cases, advanced degrees. People in my small town feel part of the Trump base and it seems like a good thing. The president goes to places way out of the way where thousands of people show up to listen to him because he cares about these people who've never been listened to in their lives by any president.

I'll stop here. I know people around the table have different thoughts and feelings about what I have said but I appreciate so much, Charles and Elizabeth, the opportunity to say something I've wanted to say for the last three years."

<u>Elizabeth, the hostess, added</u>: It had been hard for her to find the right words but as Charles's sister spoke, she was able to gather her thoughts enough to respond.

"Julie, that took so much courage to say. You know I've been a Democrat my whole life, as was my family before I met Charles. But what feels so much more important today is that we can come together and speak about what is on our minds in a truthful and honest manner. What could be more important? I can't say I understand the mindset of the people in your community and others who are proud to be part of the Trump base. What I *don't* think is that over 40 percent of the people in this country are crazy—as some extreme left-wing people have suggested. Yes, there are things that divide us, but if we can sit down and talk about our differences in a respectful manner, recognizing we each have the right to believe what we do, we might be able to look at the list of the first two or three things that we disagree about, and begin to sort through our differences. Thank you all for listening, that was a long spiel on my part but I'm so appreciative of Julie for taking the risk to say things she said, in what must feel like hostile territory at times."

<u>Jake, Kelly's first cousin, went next</u>: "Well, this is unlike any Thanksgiving meal I can remember, at least in recent times. This is odd coming from me—but I'm kind of speechless. Since you know I'm working for Bernie's campaign, you also know I might disagree with everyone who spoke so far. I believe in Bernie and everything he stands for—but listening to the discussion so far, I realize that if we don't find out why so many people stand by Donald Trump, we're

dead in the water. I might as well start looking for another job Monday morning. I now realize we can't just write these people off as kooks. Julie is certainly not a kook. I've known her for 35 years and love and respect her as my sister-in-law. I have realized just tonight that my obligation as a campaign worker for Bernie is to find out specifically why people believe in Donald Trump, why they voted for him originally, and why they are likely to vote for him again."

<u>Allyson, Kelly's sister, jumped in:</u> A senior at an Ivy League school, Allyson was a Democrat with very strong views, but seemed struck by the tenor of the conversation.

"Wow, guys, this sounds like my philosophy classes rather than a discussion about Donald Trump. You all know that I've taken time off from school to work for the Warren campaign. We all love the woman. She's spirited, energetic and has spent so much time with every individual she meets. It's remarkable. What I have to admit is that I never really spent time thinking about the Trump base. I've written them off. I guess I think they're like evangelicals who are following their leader—though I know that Trump isn't religious. I thought his people were without minds of their own, blindly following him to the edge of the cliff and beyond. Some of my professors are old enough to remember Jonestown and Jim Jones. They've recounted the story of hundreds of people poisoning themselves because they believed in what one man said. They've likened Trump to Jones, and we've all talked about people without spines following a man who projects charm, authority, power and faux concern. But I have to say, despite considering myself an educated woman, I haven't ever stopped to think about why so many people still support Trump. I don't know if I will ever understand it, but I have to give it a try. It is the only fair thing I can do if I'm going to work for a presidential contender who is challenging him. Rather than listening to what I hear on TV and read in liberal newspapers, I'm going to do my own research. I'm going to talk to Trump supporters to see what they have to say."

<u>Lyle was the last person to speak (some guests just listened, they didn't say anything):</u> "Well, since Kelly and I have been engaged, I've tried to keep a low profile at these gatherings. You all know I work on the Hill, but even so, I haven't gotten into politics much here because I want to be part of this family. Since we're being honest and Charles and Elizabeth have given us all this rare opportunity, I'll tell you where I stand. I went to Washington to work for a Republican senator who I really admire, but I've been disillusioned; not just by the Senate but by the current state of affairs in Washington. I thought we could get so much done, pass bills that could really make a difference for our country. I believed in the "Make America Great Again" idea. Now I'm seriously considering going back home to run the family business. Kelly and I haven't decided yet where we want to settle down and raise our children, but I know it will be in a place where values matter. In Washington, those ideals seem to have faded away. I'm personally on the fence about President Trump these days and have been thrown off by the impeachment hearings against him.

It's unsettling to see how partisan the House and Senate are these days. What they need is to adopt what Charles and Elizabeth created here today. A space where all ideas can be discussed without fear of losing a job or a relationship with a loved one. I've been hesitant to talk this way before, because I know most of the people in this family are Democrats. But since I'm going to be part of the family, I want to thank you, Charles and Elizabeth, for providing me with a unique opportunity to share my true feelings in a safe place where I don't feel threatened or judged. Once I have time to think things through, I will do what truly represents who I am as a person, regardless of my party affiliation or the current partisanship that exists on the Hill. If I lose my job, then so be it. Nothing in the world of work feels better than being true to myself. Now I know what has been buried in my mind because I thought I would be ostracized, must be discussed. I can't continue to play both sides in order to appease anyone."

When Lyle was finished speaking, Charles and Elizabeth raised their glasses and toasted their daughter's fiancé, while others cheered and some cried. What was clear in that moment is that people with different beliefs can come together to discuss opposing views, even very controversial topics, if respect for the opinions of others with whom they disagree can be heard without judging those who do not share similar views. Tensions that exist between and among people cannot be ignored. They must be discussed to heal wounds of the past so that a new understanding can be reached wherein respecting the right of others to have opposing opinions is valued above all else.

Guidelines for nurturing respectful conversations

1. Let people know the ground rules. As in the case of Charles and Elizabeth's Thanksgiving invitation, the instructions don't have to be complex. Something that resembles the statement

included in "The Invitation of the Future" is a good model. Make needed adjustments based on the event at hand. Here it is again:

"This year we invite you to discuss current events and political developments in your part of the world, as well as your views about our current leaders. We ask that you listen to the views of others in a respectful way. We do not expect our guests to agree on controversial topics, but request that we all appreciate the rights of others to have differing views."

2. Choose someone ahead of time who can serve as a mediator in case a particular guest fails to follow the guidelines. If that individual is not one of the hosts, make sure the designated person knows how to get someone who starts to cross a boundary back on track. If such a person starts to wade into territory that begins to sound disrespectful to another person, the mediator might suggest something that nudges him or her back to more respectful language. The following suggestion may help:

"Let's remember the guidelines of our discussion. We don't have to agree with each other, but everyone has a right to his or her opinion. Jessica, you were saying..."

3. If a guest veers way out of line, you may have to ask the person to take a break from the conversation. This can be done by the host or someone else who has previously been identified as someone who can help out if a person participating in the discussion is rude or disrespectful to another guest. Make sure the person who is to fulfill this role knows ahead of time that he or she may be needed. That person might make a statement as follows:

"Hey Jake, let's take a break. Let's go down to the family room and see what's going on with the game." Once in a neutral space, when appropriate, it can be useful if the person helping you manage guests says something like, "I see how invested you are in your point of view and I understand how strongly you feel about your opinion, but our hosts, Jack and Sally, are trying to do something different here. They're trying to give everyone a chance to voice his or her opinion without feeling intimidated." If the person who made the remarks seems to understand how he or she crossed a boundary, the assisting person may suggest that they return to the group. If that's not the case, it may be best for the person in question to stay where they are until the original discussion is over. This person may need more time to understand the concept of allowing others to have their own opinions without disparaging them.

4. On rare occasions it may be necessary to suggest that a guest needs to go home if he or she becomes belligerent. This can be awkward but it's important to protect other people who you have invited to your home. If it's a holiday weekend, for example, and the person is a guest in your home, it may be easy enough to suggest that they retire for the night. In a case like this, the person may be acting disrespectful because he or she has had too much to drink. A good night's sleep may bring clarity to the situation by the next day. If the person is not staying in your home but needs to leave, it might be optimal to either ask someone to drive him or her to the place where they are staying if they are from out of town or home if they live in the area. Calling an Uber or taxi may be appropriate as well if you believe the person has had too much to drink. No matter how things go that night, it is important to address this issue with the person in question at another time. If asking your guest to retire for the night or go to another location, the host might say something like one of the following things.

"Allyson, I think you need to take a break for the evening. You seem really upset or angry. I think it is best if you turn in for the night. You know where you're staying upstairs. We can talk about this in the morning."

If you think the person needs to or has planned to stay elsewhere one might say something like, "Allyson, I think you need a break for the evening since you appear to be angry and unable to discuss what happened. Sally and Jane (or an Uber or taxi) can take you to your hotel. We can talk about this later."

For more ideas about how to handle difficult situations such as the ones outlined above, go to www.aftermath-trump.com.

Chapter Nine

Helping a Country Heal: Reconciliation and Reparative Leadership in Rwanda

Though certainly challenging, healing is possible, and it's been done in situations far more fraught than when one person's politics differ from someone else's political worldview. Through mentalization and by "taking back" projections, repair can occur. And while it doesn't happen as frequently as one might like, it certainly does happen, and sometimes in the unlikeliest of circumstances. One place this occurred was in Rwanda. After the 1994 genocide where an estimated one million people were slaughtered, those Hutus and Tutsis who survived managed to reconcile and work together to rebuild their country.

This chapter focuses on repair in groups, a complicated concept to grapple with and a difficult process to implement, mainly because it requires participants to "take back projections." One way to think about changing the mindset of a group of people is to consider Melanie Klein's positions, which in this case involve a shift from the paranoid-schizoid position wherein people project unwanted aspects of their group onto another group. In the second position, the depressive position, that which has been projected is now "owned" in new ways by those who originally needed to cast off intolerable aspects of their group.

While daunting, the taking back of projections can be achieved with the right kind of leadership. When massive aggression is absorbed by someone in authority who can metabolize these feelings and "give them back" in a more acceptable and less affectively charged manner, change can occur.

This process took place after the Rwandan genocide: vast amounts of residual aggression were transfigured by leaders who helped people deal with their rage in acceptable ways that led to reconciliation. This demonstrated a shift from the paranoid-schizoid position to the depressive position and allowed former enemies to come together to repair their severely damaged relationships. There are also situations where repair failed, notably between the Turks and the Armenians after the Armenian Genocide of 1918.

I believe these examples capture precisely the work that we will have to undertake, and the traps that we will have to avoid, in order to heal from the Trump Presidency. And what could happen if we fail to act. [190]

Individuals changing their attitudes and behaviors towards others is, thankfully, both feasible, and relatively common, especially when a person seeks help from a professional therapist. But abusive actions by a group of people against another group of people, as in large-scale terrorism or genocide, are significantly harder to prevent, eliminate, and heal from, for a vast number of reasons. Animosity in groups *can* be repaired, I believe, its impact mitigated or reversed through the application of the principles inherent in the integrative process of mentalization on the self-exile that goes hand in hand with projective identification. If we can find a way to process community aggression, persuading groups to "own" their aggression, and in the process let go of what is lost or cannot be, then we can work together to rehabilitate relationships and truly accept and honor the rights of others. This is a critical step in nurturing connection and respect with other people.

Political, religious, and other cultural leaders, as well as other people with the power to forge relationships and implement change

---

190. A version of the ideas here first appeared in Messina, K. *Misogyny, Projective Identification, and Mentalization: Psychoanalytic, Social, and Industrial Manifestations.* Abingdon, Oxon and New York, NY: Routledge. (2019).

on a community or nationwide level, such as diplomats, can look to the essential components of projective identification and mentalization as they help people metabolize aggression on a large scale. Using these tools, group members can be persuaded to "own" their aggression and move forward from the actions that, though they cannot be erased, can be acknowledged and integrated.

Political scientist and psychoanalytic theorist C. Fred Alford has conceptualized the approach of the Frankfurt School, a group of social theorists working post-WWII and post-Holocaust, using what he termed the "four Rs": "Remembrance of those who suffered; Reparation for their loss; Reformation of reason; and Reconciliation with nature."[191]

Notably, "remorse" is not on this list of key goals. In Alford's view, raw emotion, including regret for past actions, is not useful; rather, the commitment to look forward and devise new ways to act—while keeping the past in mind—are what make all the difference. Change is possible if one embarks on remembering, repairing, reforming, and reconciling while keeping in mind the harm done to others past and present, and making amends for one's own errors in a thoughtful manner as one gradually reconciles with all aspects of what it means to be human.

The Reparative Leader

Applying the theories of Melanie Klein to groups, Alford describes what he calls "reparative leadership."[192] A responsible political leader has the ability to recognize that it is not only the aggressive urges of their enemy that the public fears, it also fears its own

---

191. C. Fred Alford, *Melanie Klein and critical social theory: An account of politics, art, and reason based on her psychoanalytic theory.* Chelsea, 1989. 170

192. Ibid. 89-90.

collective aggressive urges. Emphasizing the "goodness" of their own group and the "badness" of the other does not serve the reparative leader; finger-pointing and villainizing one's competitors and critics by characterizing them as an "evil empire" only encourages projection and reinforces division.

Alford characterizes the reparative leader as someone who sees his or her opponents as part of a shared moral or ethical whole. Because they are seen as belonging, the opposition is also seen as part of the good, and therefore can't be conveniently characterized as an evil "other." The reparative leader also questions his own group's claim to goodness, and refrains from demonizing others as a way to bolster or protect his leadership and the unity of his group. His leadership is more supple and is based upon an inclusive and flexible interpretation of the opposing group's moral tradition. Their views are not, however, utterly remade in a way that denies the opponent's otherness completely. Mahatma Gandhi, Martin Luther King, Jr., and Nelson Mandela were all genuine reparative leaders, each with a keen ability to mentalize, they held in mind the positive attributes of their "enemies" without demanding that they give up their identities.[193]

Alford sees post-traumatic stress disorder as a cultural and political phenomenon that plagues humanity more broadly than many professionals in the field of psychiatry who view this condition from a psychological and/or medical perspective. His evidence for this view is that similar events will affect people in different cultures differently—some experiencing trauma as a result and others not, mostly depending on the traditions and community institutions for group support available in different settings. Following the 2004 Indian Ocean tsunami, for example, few Sri Lankans were "traumatized" in the Western sense. "Terrorism," in

---

193. Ibid. 90.

my view, has similarly become a cultural construct. The political diagnosis was given after 9/11, when George W. Bush declared a "war on terror" (Address to a Joint Session of Congress, 2001, September 20) as though there was a correct military response for what was essentially a centuries-old political tactic. Immediately following Bush's strategic proclamation, Muslims in the U.S. and around the world were readily demonized as terrorists by media, policy-makers, and everyday Americans alike. In the two decades since, whenever someone brings out a gun and shoots in a public place—as happened near Seattle in late 2016, in Montreal in early 2017, in pre-election Paris in late April 2017—a predictable conversation ensues focusing on "foreign" (usually dark) features.

When the terrorist is eventually revealed to be "home-grown," most often with a history of mental illness and no Arab ancestry, the media reports seem to convey an air of disappointment. When a radical jihadist has attacked the West, it is, in my view, an exercise of their own humiliation and hatred through projective identification. That lashing out has, in turn, led Europeans and Americans to demonize Muslims generally. As "Muslim" became equated with "terrorist," and many Americans subverted all individuality to a predetermined set of surface characteristics, the Trump administration and its supporters, by 2016, had found their scapegoat. They themselves were now projecting their own fears and self-hatred onto a diverse set of cultures—this was projective identification on a massive, international scale. It is my belief that there is a reason for acts of terror: aggression is a form of energy, and like any energy in the physical world, it cannot simply be destroyed. Aggression can only be redirected, contained, understood or dealt with productively within the groups of people from which it emerges. If we forego communication around the aggression, it has nowhere to go and will be projected outward in a way that affects others—sometimes mildly, sometimes moderately, and sometimes in the most devastating and destructive ways.

While powerful, self-aware leaders are indisputably in a position to make a difference in the world, where else can we look for opportunities for change? Can private individuals have meaningful and lasting impact on the same scale? By combining the four Rs with the skills inherent in mentalizing, I believe that they can. Starting by teaching individuals, and then the members of small groups, and then larger groups, I believe the route to success is imaginable, and perhaps possible.

Helping people with projected anxiety, whether on a large or small scale, has considerations for those doing the assisting. When working with people who are caught in a projective-identification process, one must be extremely resistant to becoming immobilized oneself and instead must be able to weather intense projections. Seeing them as a way of communicating, rather than a way of being, potential helpers must "take on" and metabolize massive projections without becoming destabilized.

Examples of reconciliation for groups that have been on the offense with each other are few and far between, but the way in which Rwandans came together after the 1994 genocide is an illustration of how a fractured group can heal. Following the 100-day genocide, Hutus and Tutsis were able, with a lot of professional guidance and personal commitment, to put themselves in one another's shoes—working to understand themselves and their motivation more clearly, as well as acknowledge their former enemy's previous position—and set the stage for reconciliation.[194]

194. "Rwanda: From hatred to reconciliation: The story of the 1994 Rwandan genocide told through the prism of the media, exploring their role then and today." Al Jazeera. 2015.

Hutus and Tutsis: An Example of Group Mentalization

What occurred among Hutus and Tutsis after the genocide of 1994 shows us that healing is possible, even when a route to repair seems highly unlikely. The way that groups learned to mentalize in Rwanda during the years-long reconciliation appears to be a result of Alford's "reparative leadership." Since 1994, Rwandans have rebuilt their economy and repaired their social fabric—as a unified country. There are various theories about how this transformation came about, and no doubt Paul Kagame, former Tutsi rebel commander turned national civilian president, was a key factor. UN peacekeeper Roméo Dallaire's accounts paint a picture of what I speculate to be Kagame's remarkable capacity for mentalization of others' views and his achievement of the Kleinian depressive position.[195]

Developing the capacity to mentalize is challenging, and in the case of Rwanda's citizenry post-genocide, successful unification involved a distinct set of steps. Public recognition of hard truths was an early guiding principle.[196] The country also turned to the South African Commission on Truth and Reconciliation as a model for a peaceful and prosperous future. The commission, designed by Nelson Mandela and Desmond Tutu, called for Afrikaners to admit their cruel actions in front of Black Africans.[197] Rwanda's National Unity and Reconciliation Commission has given both Hutus and Tutsis the opportunity to both ask for and grant forgiveness, as long as a person owns up to what role they played and

195. Romeo Dallaire, *Shake Hands with the Devil: The Failure of Humanity in Rwanda*. Carroll & Graf, New York. 2003.

196. Joseph Sebaranzi, *God Sleeps in Rwanda: A Journey of Transformation*, Simon & Schuster, New York, 2009.

197. Address to a Joint Session of Congress and the American People, United States Capitol, Washington, DC. September 20, 2001.

what they did. Former projections of inhumanity like indescribable violence and abuse are "taken back," and as a result, some new understanding of the previously demonized can develop, and only then is reconciliation possible. The effect of this type of highly orchestrated and bipartisan mentalization is more consequential than mere truce or armistice. It is an essential step when seeking broad and genuine commitment to end major conflicts.

After the genocide, Paul Kagame was instrumental in reinstituting *umuganda* among all Rwandans, regardless of ethnicity, as a way to heal. *Umuganda* is a process that involves people gathering and then working together to accomplish a specific, shared task and toward a common goal.[198] Similar efforts have been undertaken across the globe, for instance in Colombia in the 2017 effort to reintegrate FARC narco-guerrillas and at least two rebel groups, and prior to that in Northern Ireland with the 1998 Good Friday Agreement. John Trimble and David Hume won the Nobel Peace Prize for their efforts toward a peaceful solution to the conflicts in Northern Ireland in 1998; President Juan Manuel Santos was awarded the Noble Peace Prize in 2016.[199]

Sometimes the simplest acts of working together across boundaries are all it takes to spur healing. In Rwanda, it was women, Hutu and Tutsi both, who had been victims far more often than they had been killers. Bearing this burden of intrapsychic pain, they knew they had to choose between holding onto their grief mindset for many years—perhaps indefinitely—or else move on. The ubiquitous craft of Rwandan basketry, emblematic of the citizenry's deep, shared roots, was one of the most successful ways in which they chose to heal, creating workshops, reviving traditional

198. Sigri, *Rewarding Rwanda*. Umuganda-Community Service. April 7, 2001.

199. Nicholas Casey, "Colombia's President, Juan Manuel Santos, Is Awarded Nobel Peace Prize," *The New York Times*, October 8, 2016.

designs, and marketing their products as widely as possible to spark commerce in their seriously embattled economy.[200] Real social advancement—on a personal and collective level—resulted from the commitment to a common project.

Focusing on the promise of a better future while acknowledging the atrocities of the past seems to have led to a remarkable outcome; the Rwandan transformation since the 1994 genocide has been pretty amazing when one considers how many other places in the world have stayed mired in conflict, warring psychologically or in actual combat, for seemingly limitless periods of time.

The manner in which the Rwandan government conceived of the justice and reconciliation process as a way to overcome factional divisions was nothing short of monumental. Efforts focused on bringing about a holistic culture so that its people could become, first and foremost, "Rwandan," and today, the idea of "Rwandan-ness" is embraced almost universally. By 2015, the Rwanda Reconciliation Barometer, a national survey that tracks the success of reconciliation efforts, showed that 96.7% of Rwandans affirm that "there is shared sense of national identity and inclusive citizenship in Rwanda."[201] In every subsequent year, the history of those years of conflict among the Tutsi, Hutu, and Twa fades even further into the mist.[202]

There are many successful stories of individuals overcoming past hostilities and hatred, few as inspiring as one recounted by Ms. Odile Katese's group of Tutsi and Hutu women who formed

---

200. L.J. Seymour, "Rwandans Weave Baskets of Hope," *The New York Times*, October 11, 2007.

201. NURC. *Rwanda Reconciliation Barometer.* Kigali, Rwanda (2015). http://www .genocideresearchhub.org.rw/document/rwanda-reconciliation-barometer-2015-2/

202. P. Tumwebaze, "Remarkable Changes: Rwanda." *The New York Times*, April 7, 2010.

the Ingoma Nishya ("New Drum" or "New Kingdom") drumming troupe. For many years following the genocide, Tutsi and Hutu avoided participating mutually in any cause, so the unity expressed was novel.[203] Prior to Katese forming Ingoma Nishya, drumming was an activity reserved for men. However, the new troupe not only gave the women a forum for music; more importantly, it was a vehicle for healing for the women who had been raped and mutilated in battles between the Hutu and Tutsi. Inspired to keep providing spaces where people could feel safe again, free of fear and hatred, Katese founded the first organic ice cream shop in the town of Butare. Inzozi Nziza ("Sweet Dreams") is owned and operated by a cooperative consisting of the Ingoma Nishya drummers. After getting off to a slow start, the women persevered. They got an interview on a radio station with a popular male drummer from Burundi that increased the visibility of their performing art as well as the sales in their ice cream shop.[204] This series of decisions and actions highlights the importance of taking charge, even when it is unclear what the results of one's efforts will be. We can wait for others to step forward to do what is needed to make essentials changes, but at some point someone needs to take the lead by organizing a small group of people to inspire others to change.

An example from West Timor, far from Africa, underscores the potential benefits of group mentalization. When the local government approved marble extraction companies to mine on Mutis Mountain, indigenous women (the traditional land-owners) from the Molo tribe resisted what would be the sure

---

203. M. Arlin, "Honoring Odile Gakire Katese," *Global Citizen*, 2011.

204. M. Yerman, "Sweet Dreams: Reconciliation in Rwanda at DocNYC," *Huffington Post*, November 12. 2012.

devastation of the sacred source of all the rivers on the island. As forest clearing and digging began in 1996, Aleta Baun and three colleagues visited countless villages to urge their people to remember the significance of the threat: the mountain is their body, its rivers their blood, its forest their hair, was the powerful message they disseminated. Moreover, its plants provided an important part of their economic and social lives—the dyes used in indigenous women's weaving. Ten years later, in 2006, 100 women went to a quarry, formed their looms in a circle, and performed a silent "weaving occupation" for more than a year. They persisted. [205]

Radical change between groups in opposition rarely happens in such a short period of time. Rather, animosity and hatred between rival groups is more often seen to last for hundreds of years or more. For instance, shortly after the prophet Muhammed died in the sixth century, a fractious Sunni–Shia ideological conflict over the authenticity of Muhammad's successor began—and endures today. Another longstanding failed reconciliation is still occurring between the Turks and the Armenians. Acknowledgment of the genocide in Armenia that occurred more than 103 years ago has been suppressed or denied since it took place. Turkey, as well as a handful of other countries that fear reprisals from the Turkish government, continues to deny the genocide. But the Armenian people and their descendants have never forgotten the events that occurred beginning on April 24, 1915, and in 2018, thousands of demonstrators amassed in Los Angeles near Little Armenia to celebrate the 103rd anniversary of the Armenian genocide. Marches organized by the Unified Young Armenians included

---

205. G. Merlino. "Aleta Baun Protects her Timor Indonesian Homeland." *Eden Keeper.* December 9, 2014.

participants who waved flags and called for the US government to officially recognize the atrocities. [206]

My hypothesis is that the Turkish state, and many of its citizens, have never "taken back" the projections they have historically put onto the Armenians in the form of denialism. Repair has not been possible because of this massive denial—as of this writing, the Turkish government still officially denies that the genocide occurred (the United States officially recognized the genocide in 2019). Without this recanting, there is no possibility of healing, and disparagement, hatred, and animosity will continue to prevail. Perhaps only a change in leadership in Turkey will set the tone for change.

206. J.C. Klemack, "Flag-Waving Marchers in Los Angeles Demand Recognition of Armenian Genocide," NBC News. April 24. 2018.

Looking Beyond 2020:
Moving Past This Moral Morass

Since the earliest years of the republic, the United States has rarely faced challenges as serious as those that confronted us in 2020. A sorely mishandled global pandemic which culminated in hundreds of thousands dead and a severely weakened economy, combined with a critical climate crisis and fractured foreign policy, have left Americans as vulnerable as they have ever been. But we will move forward. As Harry S. Truman said, "America was built on courage, on imagination, and an unbeatable determination to do the job at hand." That is the American way.

But how to do that job? The path ahead is hardly smooth. To successfully move past the uniquely alarming mixture of chaos, distrust, and hostility of the past four years calls for enormous change in both behavior and mindset, individually and as a country. We've got a lot of work to do if we want to become better citizens and neighbors; there is no quick fix to healing the divide and resuming civil discourse. Above all, we must be courageous in our willingness to look beyond our own siloed groups of like-minded people.

And it will take a certain type of president to show us how to make these strides: one with not only essential leadership qualities like experience, commitment, and intellectual acuity, but someone with a broader, perhaps less heavily lauded set of attributes. We need a leader who embodies the characteristics that we want to emulate in our own lives.

Who can lead us out of this mess?

Here, I offer a sketch of an ideal presidential political candidate and the personality traits he or she might possess, no matter the party affiliation.

Gifted presidential historians from Robert Caro and Doris Kearns Goodwin to Bob Woodward have plumbed hindsight to assess what great governance demands in a leader, dedicating thousands of pages to examining the specific ideals, temperament, and behaviors that combine to make a great president.

A leading takeaway for Caro is that power is a litmus test of character. "Power reveals," he says. "When a leader gets enough power, when he doesn't need anybody anymore [...] then we can see how he always wanted to treat people, and we can also see—by watching what he does with his power—what he wanted to accomplish all along."[207] When a leader uses their power to truly benefit others, rather than to simply build up more and more political capital, a special integrity is unveiled.

But what are the specific characteristics behind this kind of integrity? Among several—including humility, grace, self-discipline, and the critical blend of realism and idealism that so many former U.S. presidents have relied on in times of crisis—are two that I believe will be the key to emerging from the crippling divisions and misunderstandings that are threatening our future: openness and empathy.

Openness boils down to the ability to listen and learn. A president who regards others as worthy of paying attention to, and then carefully weighs what they are seeing and hearing, is a leader

---

207. Diane Coutu, "Lessons in Power: Lyndon Johnson Revealed," *Harvard Business Review.* (Cambridge, Mass.: April 2006), https://hbr.org/2006/04/lessons-in-power-lyndon -johnson-revealed.

who is setting him or herself up for success. No one can be an expert on everything. Especially important is a leader's insistence on the views and knowledge of experts. We are in dire need of a commander in chief who not only surrounds him or herself with people who have the best, most pertinent, information, but who also goes to the necessary lengths to preserve and protect their findings and assessments.

The ability to look objectively at facts—even unpleasant facts—and not be paralyzed by ominous news or deluded by wishful thinking is vital to capable leadership. It's this kind of strength that earned praise for leaders like Prime Minister Jacinda Ardern in New Zealand and New York Governor Andrew Cuomo for their handling of the coronavirus in the earliest stages of the pandemic.

Openness is closely related to honesty. Honesty can make or break communication between leaders and the people who depend on their guidance. To be clear, honesty does not automatically mean sharing every bit of information possible—presidents and others tasked and burdened with exceptional power often need to tailor the release of information in order to protect their countries' interests—but it does mean communicating information when it is relevant and useful to do so by disclosing it in a timely fashion.

Without honesty, trustworthiness declines precipitously, and a leader rapidly descends into the quagmire of evasion and chaos that we find ourselves witnessing at this moment in history. Being led by an individual who refuses to take ownership of anything and actively spurns personal or institutional responsibility is not just personally disheartening—it is scary and dangerous. Letting a pandemic rage unabated across the country is a terrifying relinquishment of duty. Denying human impact on the global climate crisis is a domestic and foreign policy risk of serious consequence. Both are immeasurably grave in their potential cost to human lives.

Only when a leader puts in the effort to listen to others without cutting them off, silencing them, or worse, belittling their views, can that person then practice the other leadership trait I believe essential to moving forward from our present situation: empathy.

Throughout this book, I have continuously emphasized the benefit to all of us—as individual people and also as a nation—of mentalization. The practice of listening to ideas beyond one's own, giving others the freedom to express themselves, and allowing a mutual sharing of ideas—without the pressure to come to any kind of consensus—is exactly what we need to see more of right now.

Since the founding of the United States, the idea of healing divisions through recognition of other points of view has been promoted wholeheartedly. A public servant's sense of moral purpose is often guided by something more than their aim to improve opportunity and the lives of others—it is guided by their ability to listen to diverse opinions without jumping in and quashing differences. Only when a president controls the natural impulse to jump in or take over—to "act" presidential instead of "being" presidential—and instead genuinely enables others to express themselves, will he or she be able to pursue and realize their higher purpose: acting in the best interest of others.

Postscript

I first conceived of this book out of a deep concern for the dysfunction I was witnessing around me, the worst I had seen in my decades of clinical practice as a psychoanalyst. Immediately following the 2016 presidential election, political divisions were at a new height, and that divisiveness was starting to poison our personal interactions. At the time, I never could have predicted the gravity of what would come next. The protracted descent into animosity, fear, and grief that Americans have collectively experienced over the last four years has left us confused, frustrated, and at times hopeless about how to move forward. As I wrote this book I focused on our potential for change, even under the worst circumstances. I was looking to the future, drawing on my experience to offer meaningful and practical ways to heal and move on from a chaotic, adversarial world made more so by our vulnerability to a powerful force: Donald Trump.

Events seem to march on at an unrelenting and hair trigger pace these days, especially in the period immediately leading up to a national election. As I put the final touches on this manuscript, the United States is in uncharted territory on several different fronts: epidemiologically, economically, and politically. With close to 215,000 Americans dead from Covid-19, neither a vaccine nor a cure is imminent, let alone the issuance of a set of national public health guidelines that would mitigate the spread of coronavirus. New cases are back up to where they were nearly six months ago. The economic outlook is no sunnier: more Americans have filed for unemployment in 2020 than voted for their Commander-in-Chief in 2016. [208] On the political front, we have split into factions of constituents so filled with distrust and animus that it's impossible to have a conversation, let alone a productive exchange of ideas.

The state of the union is, at this writing, a 5-alarm, Category 4, Defcon 1, emergency.

And in the middle of all this Donald Trump was hospitalized with Covid-19 following what Anthony Fauci called a "super spreader" [209] event at the White House Rose Garden to announce the nomination of a Supreme Court replacement for Ruth Bader Ginsburg. Fortune seems to have smiled on him, and he appears to be recovering (with the help of a not insignificant regimen of treatments, some of which are considered state of the art and experimental). While the world waited fitfully to see how his health would be affected, some were more attuned to other possible effects of the experience. Would changes to masking and social distancing behavior around the president finally be put into place? Would the president's demeanor be altered in any way, with him having felt firsthand the miseries of this disease that has killed so many? Would he be able to express vulnerability or empathy?

The answer to each of these questions is a resounding "no."

The upshot of Trump's brush with illness reads more like a script of his previous behaviors and activities than an indication of any sort of revelation. With Trump, what has emerged is a trend that you are either with him or against him, a familiar binary

---

208. Robert Reich, [RBReich]. Next time you hear Trump and his enablers touting the economy, remind them that more Americans have filed for unemployment this year than voted for Trump in 2016. [Tweet]. October 10, 2020. Retrieved from https://twitter.com /rbreich/status/1314923475627323393?s=27

209. Ruth Graham, "Fauci says the White House hosted a 'super spreader' event." *The New York Times*. October 9, 2020. https://www.nytimes.com/live/2020/10/09/world /covid-coronavirus

that fuels the bully in him. Witness: in-person campaign events with thousands of supporters held on the White House lawn and around the country, accusations that Gold Star families gave him the virus[210], attacks on powerful women (Kamala Harris is "a monster"[211]; Michigan Governor Gretchen Whitmer, is doing a "terrible job"[212]), and the persistent reluctance by his administration to confirm that a peaceful transition of power will not be guaranteed if Trump's opponent wins the November election.[213] I could go on.

The spot we are left in is anything but clear—as a country, and as individuals. Certainty about possible next steps will elude us until every last ballot is counted. What we do know is that whatever way the electorate goes, the country has a lot of work to do going forward. Not just in saving democracy, but also in saving our children, our planet and ourselves, for it is impossible to flourish in the state of anxiety and distrust that has prevailed over the last four years, and which was simmering earlier than that.

Things may seem irrecoverable. But this is not necessarily how the future needs to unfold. If we can learn to work together in more productive ways without recklessly casting aspersions on

210. Jennifer Steinhauer, J. "Trump Suggests Gold Star Families May Be to Blame for His Infection," *The New York Times.* October 8, 2020 https://www.nytimes.com/2020/10/08/us/politics/trump-coronavirus-gold-star-families.html

211. Maggie Astor, "Kamala Harris and the 'Double Bind' of Racism and Sexism," *The New York Times.* October 9, 2020. https://www.nytimes.com/2020/10/09/us/politics/kamala-harris-racism-sexism.html

212. Fadel Allassan, "Trump blasts Gov. Whitmer after news she was target of terror plot." Axios. October 9, 2020. https://www.axios.com/trump-gretchen-whitmer-kidnapping-plot-d6a62746-fdb0-44fd-a0f0-16bd15c55f3f.html

213. Nick Niedzwiadek, N. "Pence sidesteps question about peaceful transfer of power." Politico October 7, 2020. https://www.politico.com/news/2020/10/07/pence-vp-debate-transfer-of-power-427665

others with whom we have disagreements, a different and better America can emerge.

What is of paramount importance is the idea that we must not give up. As psychologist Viktor Frankl, a Holocaust survivor, wrote, "Forces beyond your control can take away everything you possess except one thing, your freedom to choose how you will respond to the situation." [214]

We hold in our hands the response to the "situation" of the last four years. In order for real change to occur, Fareed Zakaria is correct. As he stated on October 11, 2020 on his television show, *GPS (Global Public Square),* we all need to use our personal agency to ensure that positive change occurs.

In this book, I've attempted to present a thoughtful analysis of how we got to this new low in our interpersonal communications and have tried to provide a road map for how to repair the schisms that have emerged among us. Despite clashes in our political views and mounting tensions among us, I am hopeful that, with the right tools, we can rebuild trust and respect for one another.

Since civil exchanges have been derailed in many situations, we need to start listening to each other—really listening—not just trying to win debates or change others' opinions. If we are going to work towards collaborating with each other for the sake of ourselves, our families, and our country versus continuously disagreeing, we must to be able to tolerate what people with different opinions have to say in an atmosphere of respect.

In order to heal from the wounds of the past and repair the damage that has been done in the last four years while developing more optimal ways of interacting, we need to start treating each other with empathy and compassion rather than in vitriolic ways that breed violence and hatred.

---

214. Viktor E. Frankl, *Man's Search for Meaning.* Beacon Press Boston, Mass. 1959.

This is a tall order but one we must embrace if we are going to reengage with each other in productive ways; a choice we can still make before our ability to live in a democracy slips away.

Best wishes, and stay safe,
Karyne Messina, Ed.D.
Chevy Chase, MD; October 11, 2020

.

Lightning Source UK Ltd.
Milton Keynes UK
UKHW020640120221
378684UK00015B/1105